"*Reading the Bible Around the World* is a bold invitation to engage the biblical text with a posture of epistemic humility and hermeneutical generosity, however unfinished. Each chapter helps us develop different levels of intercultural competence through interpretive routines that guide us toward mutual belonging and co-reading the Bible. Ultimately, this work is an introduction for how to re-form our racial-patriarchal reading habits, forged through centuries of inhabiting colonial modernity spaces and identities that have formed us into self-sufficient entrepreneurs of single truths. This is a text highly recommended for the global Christian of today and tomorrow."

Oscar García-Johnson, associate professor of theology and Latinx studies at Fuller Seminary and author of *Spirit Outside the Gate*

"Biblical interpretation is undergoing a tectonic shift, from regarding Western methods and concerns as the only correct way of reading Scripture to embracing the many faithful ways of reading that are emerging from cultures around the world. I cannot imagine a more skillful, hospitable, and accessible introduction to the expanding conversation than this remarkable volume. This is biblical interpretation in the form of dialogue rather than debate, with each participant offering treasures both old and new from the storehouses of their cultures. I look forward to the conversations it will generate in the classroom."

L. Daniel Hawk, Ashland Theological Seminary

"Wow, finally a book that explores different interpretations of Old and New Testament readings from the perspectives of marginalized communities. To think that the invisible and voiceless can widen our lens of these readings! I can tell you that *Reading the Bible Around the World* will surprise you at every turn. Since technology has made our world smaller, this is a must-read for scholars, ministers, laity, and chaplains who are ready to embrace a deeper understanding of how diverse constituencies read, interpret, and live out their understanding of the Bible."

Joanne Rodríguez, executive director of the Hispanic Theological Initiative

T0243706

READING THE BIBLE AROUND THE WORLD

A STUDENT'S GUIDE TO GLOBAL HERMENEUTICS

FEDERICO ALFREDO ROTH,
JUSTIN MARC SMITH,
KIRSTEN SONKYO OH,
ALICE YAFEH-DEIGH, AND
KAY HIGUERA SMITH

IVP
Academic

An imprint of InterVarsity Press
Downers Grove, Illinois

InterVarsity Press
P.O. Box 1400 | Downers Grove, IL 60515-1426
ivpress.com | email@ivpress.com

InterVarsity Press® is the publishing division of InterVarsity Christian Fellowship/USA®. For more information, visit intervarsity.org.

Scripture quotations, unless otherwise noted, are from the New Revised Standard Version Bible, copyright © 1989 National Council of the Churches of Christ in the United States of America. Used by permission. All rights reserved worldwide.

The publisher cannot verify the accuracy or functionality of website URLs used in this book beyond the date of publication.

Cover design and image composite: David Fassett
Interior design: Jeanna Wiggins

ISBN 978-1-5140-0186-8 (print) | ISBN 978-1-5140-0187-5 (digital)

Printed in the United States of America ♾

Library of Congress Cataloging-in-Publication Data
Names: Roth, Federico Alfredo, author.
Title: Reading the Bible around the world : a student's guide to global
   hermeneutics / Federico Alfredo Roth, Justin Marc Smith, Kirsten Sonkyo
   Oh, Alice Yafeh-Deigh, Kay Higuera Smith.
Description: Downers Grove, IL : InterVarsity Press, [2022] | Includes
   bibliographical references and index.
Identifiers: LCCN 2022019798 (print) | LCCN 2022019799 (ebook) | ISBN
   9781514001868 (print) | ISBN 9781514001875 (digital)
Subjects: LCSH: Bible–Criticism, interpretation, etc. |
   Bible–Hermeneutics. | Globalization–Religious aspects–Christianity.
Classification: LCC BS511.3 .R675 2022 (print) | LCC BS511.3 (ebook) |
   DDC 220.6–dc23/eng/20220615
LC record available at https://lccn.loc.gov/2022019798
LC ebook record available at https://lccn.loc.gov/2022019799

29 28 27 26 25 24 23 22 | 8 7 6 5 4 3 2 1

FEDERICO A. ROTH

For my mother, Maria Renée Trujillo

JUSTIN MARC SMITH

For Malcolm Xavier, Theodore Jaymes Dewitt, and

Naima Justine Gail. For my wife, Jayme Nicole Smith.

For my father, Freddy Lee Smith

KIRSTEN SONKYO OH

To my parents, Hannah Young Han and Joseph Pyong Oh.

You have instilled a deep love for the Scriptures and

the relational God revealed in those texts.

ALICE YAFEH-DEIGH

To Donalice, Ariel, and Johaness,

without whom this would not be possible

For the students of Azusa Pacific University,

whose generous curiosity, enthusiasm for learning,

and trust in us as their faculty have inspired these pages

CONTENTS

1

INTRODUCTION

WHY WE NEED GLOBAL APPROACHES

JUSTIN MARC SMITH

"Who am I?" "How do I self-define?" At various points in our lives, we must consider these questions of identity. Sometimes we are at a loss to know who we are. Sometimes our self-definition is crystal clear and unavoidable. Sometimes we don't take the time to assess ourselves in this way, and even worse, we often live lives so crowded with the noise and expectations of the day-to-day that we have no time or space to ask these important questions. So, maybe, we just don't know. We don't know who we are, and we have never taken the time to think about it. As we begin together, we want to offer a caution about being so unaware: unaware of ourselves, unaware of our surroundings, unaware of the social structures at play, and unaware of our own social location. Who we are (where we come from, our social values, our culture[s], our language[s], our customs, our worldview[s]) shapes how we see and experience the world. Sometimes this shapes us in very powerful and overt ways, and at other times it shapes us in ways that we never see or know. Often, as readers and interpreters, we are almost incapable of seeing others and ourselves in new (and helpful) ways without some seismic shift (this is especially true for those who exist in spheres of power and privilege).

This might be better understood through an illustration. Imagine two students, with one standing on a desk in the middle of the room and the other sitting on the floor under the desk, or so close to the desk that the desk is all the student can see. Now, ask the first student to describe what they see. The student on the desk will describe the room and the view their position on the desk affords them. They will describe the lights and the items on the wall and how the other students look to them. Now, ask the student seated on the floor near or under the desk what they see. They cannot help but describe the desk. The desk is their reality. It is what is in front of them, and it is the thing that prevents them from seeing and experiencing the room to the fullest. The student standing on the desk rarely describes the desk. They take the desk for granted. The desk just is; it is a part of how they are able to see and experience the room. All of this is well and good for the student on the desk, but what about the other student? Who we are and what social location we inhabit radically shapes our experience of the world and of others. Given this difference in points of view, who in this illustration is better positioned to discuss the desk and the way it can be limiting for some? How might we move from "desked" experience to "shared" experience?[1]

STOP AND THINK

- Who are you? How do you self-define?
- What traditions are important to you and your family?
- Who would you be if those traditions or cultural identity markers were removed? What if they were stripped away?

---

[1]Thanks is due here to Rev. Dr. Karen McKinney and Dr. Gregg Moder for the content of this example.

- Who do you identify with more, the student on the desk or the student under the desk?

- Why might having new perspectives be important?

EXPLORING TRADITIONS—NEW INTERPRETATIONS FOR NEW CONTEXTS

As the world becomes "smaller," the incorporation of new ideas and new approaches to reading and interpreting Scripture becomes important as we encounter people with perspectives, experiences, and cultures different from our own. One way to begin this discussion is to look at how Scripture has been read and how we might begin to read it differently. For the majority of the last thousand years, biblical studies (in its various forms) has been dominated by the voices of European and Euro-American men. There may be some criticisms to be drawn here, but our point is to suggest that there are many other people in the world (women and men), representing many diverse experiences whose voices have not been heard. In the 1970s and 1980s, many recognized that approaches to Scripture that were at home in a variety of social locations were needed. Liberative readings began to emerge that were specifically analogous and at home in Latin America, Africa, Asia, and within diasporic (those who have been dispersed) communities that had mobilized to North American and European contexts (e.g., Latin American liberation, African liberation, Asian liberation). More recently, we have begun to move beyond the ethnic and territorial boundaries that defined the prior stages. The 1990s and 2000s have witnessed the rise of various reading approaches that may be termed "minority discourse," or more broadly, contextual/global.[2]

Our current interpretive methodologies and approaches owe much of their vitality to the growing influx of non-Western intellectuals

---

[2]See A. R. JanMohamed and D. Lloyd, eds., *The Nature and Context of Minority Discourse* (Oxford: Oxford University Press, 1990). See further Fernando F. Segovia, "Minority Studies and Christian Studies," in *A Dream Unfinished: Theological Reflections on America from the Margins*, ed. Eleazar S. Fernandez and Fernando F. Segovia (Maryknoll, NY: Orbis, 2001), 1-33.

moving into Western academic settings. These scholars have both expanded and disrupted normative expectations for what constitutes business-as-usual biblical interpretation. They have done so by featuring as central to their work increasingly specified issue-, identity-, and gender-based commitments. Those who craft and use such specialized approaches often hail from subaltern populations at home in *both* the First and Third World. An appreciation for new and emerging contexts will continue requiring new and emerging ways of reading and interpreting Scripture.

STOP AND THINK

- What is exciting about new approaches to interpreting Scripture?

- What concerns you? How might you work through or resolve these concerns?

EXPLORING TRADITIONS—HOW HAVE WE STUDIED/INTERPRETED THE BIBLE IN THE PAST?

Where do we begin when exploring how we have studied the Bible in the past? We can talk about how the first writers and hearers/interpreters of the biblical texts read and interpreted them. We can also talk about how the texts have been read and interpreted by both Jewish and Christian communities over time. But our focus here is on how biblical scholars of the *contemporary* era have read and interpreted Scripture.

The practice of using historical-critical methodologies dominated biblical interpretation, in professional spheres, from at least the middle of the nineteenth century through to the midpoint of the twentieth century. As advanced by scholars in Euro-American circles, the overriding concern of historical criticism was to decipher what a given text *meant* rather than to determine what it may *mean*. For historical criticism, what the interpreter reads in the Bible cannot be taken at face value. *Rather, the Bible is much like a window through which the skilled exegete looks to see a world behind.* The act of peering through this "window" correctly is strenuous work that entails the need for highly trained readers with a set of honed technical skills. Led predominantly by American and European scholars, historical critics developed specific and interrelated areas of expertise (e.g., textual, source, redaction, and form criticism). A principal aim of this so-called higher criticism was to initially fragment the biblical text into its basic literary layers and sources. Only by unraveling the biblical material could its various threads be isolated, identified, labeled, and examined on their own. The task of historical critics was one of seeking to identify the earliest, and therefore most genuine, form of the biblical text.

The historical-critical method asserted that meaning could be retrieved in the form of history. In this way, the method was meant to illuminate a particular text's life-setting, its original audience, and its original meaning to that audience. In order to achieve the discovery of historical meaning, the interpreter was required to treat the received text as the raw material for further, more rigorous, interpretation or exegesis. In so doing, historical criticism considered the biblical texts in ways reminiscent of an archaeologist surveying a landscape. The Bible was to be excavated. Only through the implementation of measurable and quantifiable skills could the biblical scholar rightly sift through its literary layers. Moreover, only by employing such skills could the world of the text, *and thus its meaning*, be unearthed. In the end, the biblical scholar was unlike the biblical author; the biblical scholar was objective while the biblical author had a point of view or agenda. The latter recorded history into text while the former decoded text into history.

Biblical scholars of this period tended to be highly influenced by Eurocentric and male-dominated worldviews. These worldviews were firmly tied to the related concepts of impartiality and specialization.

Only those who were enculturated in the worldview of the European Enlightenment could execute unbiased and apolitical biblical interpretation. It was understood that in order to properly understand the Bible one must ascend to a certain level of autonomy and disinterestedness (lack of bias). Biblical scholarship was reserved for those who put aside personal, political, and ideological affiliations to better know the text and its world. In order to remain evenhanded, the historical critic was to maintain a certain sense of separation from the subject. Thus, the field was often limited to experts who would faithfully, if not mechanically, apply its methods. This was the hyperprofessionalized realm of philologists, archaeologists, historians, and the like.

However, these approaches were rarely satisfactory in telling the entire story of Scripture. History had (and has) its limitations. Other scholars in the contemporary era have desired to encounter the words of the biblical text in different ways. Through these, new advancements were made in the field of literary theory as it related to the reading and interpretation of biblical texts. Perhaps the most important advancement was that, with the advent of literary theory, biblical scholars began moving away from talking about "methods."

Literary theory seeks to examine and understand the world of the text, or the text itself. The concern here is with the vocabulary, the setting, the structure, the characters, and any of the various literary characteristics of the text itself. The mechanistic and impersonal meanings of the text were being abandoned as the field began dialoguing in more relaxed terms, that is, in terms of "approaches" to reading texts. This led to a gradual rethinking of meaning's location. Meaning could no longer be found exclusively in the interchange between ancient authors and their audience(s). Meaning could also reside in the reality of the text, that is, within the boundaries drawn by the language of the text itself.[3]

---

[3]Leo G. Perdue, *The Collapse of History: Reconstructing Old Testament Theology* (Eugene, OR: Wipf and Stock, 1994), 153-54, 187-88.

However, the reader was still called to supreme levels of specialization. Only those who could employ modern literary theory could appropriately analyze ancient writings. By requiring such skills, the methods of higher criticism were replaced with those of literary techniques. The end result of interpretation endured; only the processes were exchanged. *Meaning was still located solely in the text.* Interpretation remained an endeavor in which the text yielded its significance to all *academically trained* readers. As with their historical-critical colleagues, literary interpreters were ideally without presuppositions, sociocultural or theological dimensions, and neutral.[4] The concerns of flesh-and-blood readers undoubtedly began to emerge in the shift toward literary theory. However, this approach privileged only an idealized and formally trained reader. The recognition that all readers are socially located would come about in a subsequent wave of biblical studies.

STOP AND THINK

- What are *historical-critical* methodologies?

- What are the strengths and weaknesses of this approach to reading the Bible?

- What did *literary approaches* to the Bible seek to accomplish?

- What issues do these approaches raise? Concerns?

EXPLORING TRADITIONS—TAKING SOCIAL LOCATION OF THE READER INTO ACCOUNT

The advancements in literary theory were not alone in shifting interpretive approaches away from rigid historical criticism. The fields of cultural and social-scientific criticism were instrumental in moving the conversation regarding biblical interpretation forward in the

---

[4]Fernando F. Segovia, *Decolonizing Biblical Studies: A View from the Margins* (Maryknoll, NY: Orbis, 2000), 20.

1960s and 1970s. This movement was more at home in the wider field of the humanities. Rather than engaging in theological discussion, cultural criticism turned to economic, sociological, and anthropological theories.[5] Cultural criticism understood the biblical text to be a product of its unique times, with specific social and cultural dimensions everywhere evident. These approaches addressed "questions of social class and class conflict—applicable across time and cultures and hence addressed from a broad comparative perspective; questions of social institutions, roles, and behavior."[6]

These new approaches and the questions they raised are important. Often biblical scholars (and students) are unaware of the social systems to which they belong, and they tend to miss crucial data or interpret information in terms of prevailing (and often restrictive) Euro-American intuitions.[7] Interpretation becomes a hazardous project whenever readers fail to account for the fact that ancient documents (e.g., biblical texts) rely on distinctive sets of cultural assumptions that cannot be accessed through sophisticated guesswork. Instead of relying on intuition, and despite its inherent limitations, social-science methodology advocates that interpreters use contemporary models of human relations. Such study forms templates for understanding human interactions in the ancient world.[8] This approach seeks to bridge the gap between the contemporary reader and the world of the text by providing the necessary crosscultural tools for understanding the societal framework in which the original discourse took place.[9] Simply put, this approach considers the cultural differences at play within the world of the text and within the world of the contemporary reader. Thus, as we as current readers are more in tune with our own social and cultural locations, the better we will be able

---

[5]Segovia, *Decolonizing Biblical Studies*, 22-23.
[6]Segovia, *Decolonizing Biblical Studies*, 24.
[7]Segovia, *Decolonizing Biblical Studies*, 12.
[8]Bruce J. Malina, "The Social Sciences and Biblical Interpretation," in *The Bible and Liberation: Political and Social Hermeneutics*, ed. Norman K. Gottwald (Maryknoll, NY: Orbis, 1983), 11.
[9]Malina, "Social Sciences," 13.

to navigate the key cultural differences that make reading and interpreting both difficult and possible.

Here is an example: think about the story of Israel as recorded in the Hebrew Bible. What are the key issues at stake? What are the overarching cultural concerns? How might our reading of Israel change if we understood Israel through the cultural perspective of a commitment to its liberation from Egyptian and Canaanite domination?[10] What if, rather than focusing on the Hebrew Bible solely as a record of actual events, or as a warehouse of history as tradition, we saw it as the expression of Israel's struggle against oppressive forces? How might that open up new ways for us to read and interpret Scripture? In what ways might we envision this approach opening up new ways to read and interpret the other texts of the Christian canon? Yes, Scripture is historical, and it is couched in history, but it is (and can be) so much more than a dusty historical document with a meaning that is fixed somewhere in the past. Instead, it can be (and is) a text that continues to have new (and valuable) meanings as we encounter it in new and innovative ways.

STOP AND THINK

- What are the benefits of *crosscultural* approaches? Are there lingering issues?
- Why is biblical interpretation so complicated? Does it have to be? Why or why not?

ACCESSING THE FULL MEANING OF SCRIPTURE— WHY GLOBAL APPROACHES MATTER

Accessing the full spectrum of meaning entails a wide array of methodological tools, as we have seen. Historical approaches are helpful but

---

[10]Norman K. Gottwald, "Sociological Method in the Study of Ancient Israel," in *The Bible and Liberation: Political and Social Hermeneutics*, rev. ed., ed. Norman K. Gottwald and Richard A. Horsley (Maryknoll, NY: Orbis, 1993), 145-46.

limited, and much the same can be said for all of the approaches mentioned above. The idealized, objective, highly trained and impartial reader that dominated the first fifty years of the twentieth century has begun to fade as the primary interpretive voice. In place of that reader, the socially located and ideologically aware reader has begun to slowly materialize. What this means is that now, all of us as readers (both students and professors) have become, and are becoming, more and more aware of our own social locations and the social locations of the writers of the biblical texts. This means that all of us have points of view and these points of view shape how we read, interpret, and experience Scripture.

While we can never rid ourselves of our own social location(s) (unlike those of the previous era who thought that we could), we *can* be aware of it/them and how it/they shape our experience of the text and others.

Contextual or global biblical studies is conceptually grouped under the broader thematic framework of cultural studies. The cultural studies model is an interdisciplinary field of study that encompasses a range of interpretive approaches. Key to this approach is the recognition that culture influences and transforms people's lived experiences and social relations. This highlights the reality that social location helps readers read the Bible in diverse ways. As such, there is a keen interest in the analysis and interpretation of the social and cultural dynamics in written works, including Scripture. Scientific objectivity or neutrality is *not the ideal in a cultural study approach.* On the contrary, what is stressed is the significance and importance of social location on the interpretive process, without the implication that interpretation is immune to being subjective. Similarly, in a thoroughgoing way, the cultural study model foregrounds the need for the contextual interpreter to be context sensitive. It challenges the interpreter to pay close attention to sociocultural, political, and religious elements of the text, while also scrutinizing how readers' contextual factors dynamically interact with their own interpretation of the text.

The objective of contextual/global approaches is to enlarge the scope of the interpretive process in order to see the world "in front" of the text. The major reformulation is found in the shift toward the current reader (or reading communities) who enjoys greater attention while the text occupies a more secondary (but vitally important) role in the construction of meaning. The reader (along with their community) is no longer called to be disinterested or universalized. The full range of their located status is considered. They are celebrated as a historically shaped, politically engaged, ethnic, gendered, racial, local, socioeducational, socioreligious, value-driven, ideological product.[11] Social awareness and commitments are to be celebrated, not denied or downplayed. In this way, contextual/global hermeneutics practice a brand of "fierce self-esteem."[12] This helps us to recognize that all biblical interpretations (good or bad, right or wrong) are conditioned by the social location of the reader.

These approaches invite readers, regardless of specialized academic skills, to peer into biblical stories for themselves. Arriving at meaning entails that readers interact with the text through the cultural/ ideological tools available to them. Readers, perhaps hailing from outside the academic sphere, and as aware members of their unique community, create relevant and meaningful interpretation. The text is understood to have multiple meanings since readers themselves have the potential to be quite diverse. Rather than searching for a definitive singular meaning, there is openness that promotes the broad spectrum of interpretive possibilities. Universalizing tendencies and once-and-for-all outcomes, which may seek to evaluate the validity of a given interpretation over another, are viewed as questionable or as outright invalid for many of these models. There are many rewards and many challenges that come with these new and varied approaches. Often over the course of this book we will be

---

[11]Segovia, *Decolonizing Biblical Studies*, 39, 47.

[12]R. S. Sugirtharajah, "Thinking About Vernacular Hermeneutics Sitting in a Metropolitan Study," in *Vernacular Hermeneutics*, ed. R. S. Sugirtharajah (Sheffield: Sheffield, 1999), 94.

asking students to stretch themselves and to grow as they encounter new (and sometimes difficult) approaches to the text. The approaches may be from cultural perspectives that are different from their own. But in encountering these new approaches, students will also encounter new opportunities for deeper engagement and understanding of the living and breathing biblical text.

CHAPTER OVERVIEWS AND IMPORTANT FEATURES

Chapter two introduces students to the hallmarks of reading approaches that originate from Latin America. We examine the diversity of this perspective while also detailing the major historical moments that have helped shape biblical interpretation and meaning-making in these regions of the world. This chapter identifies the biblical and theological centers of gravity anchoring Latina/o ways of reading. Additionally, it attends to areas of intersectionality wherein the experience of migration—which plays a prominent role for many in Latin America today—impacts Bible reading and signification.

Chapter three continues the conversation by helping readers become more fully aware of the contextual character that underpins all biblical interpretation. Its specific aim is to introduce readers to interpretive approaches at home in African contexts. It does this through a critical look at the distinctive variables, questions, and problems that are of concern for African interpreters of the Bible in general and sub-Saharan Africans in particular. Unique to this discussion is a highlighting of the presence and effects of both colonial and postcolonial realities that have shaped, and continue to shape, African engagements with biblical texts.

Chapter four introduces students to the concepts associated with the more standard and centered European/Euro-American readings of Scripture. Many students of European/Euro-American origin experience a certain lack of awareness vis-à-vis social location. As a result, their identities seem to possess a certain invisibility. This chapter seeks to remove that invisibility and present Euro-American students with the realities and challenges of reading from their own social location.

Chapter five introduces students to the particularity of reading the Bible from the Asian/Asian American perspectives. While the scope of the social location is broad, attention will especially be paid to the conscious/unconscious lens of Confucian philosophy and how it, at once, is in resonance and dissonance with Western interpretations of the Bible. Readers will be able to discern the variety of interpretations of the Bible, recognizing how the tradition and experience of each reader serves to magnify the tapestry of God's Word for the global world.

Chapter six moves beyond the geographic categories of previous chapters to highlight how globalization, migration, border crossings, and diasporas (both physical and abstract) have served to creolize Bible reading and meaning-making. Emphasis is placed on the ever-evolving identities of readers as "hybridic" and hyphenated, and thus the need for language that captures the complexities and shared categories of today's world. Additionally, the Bible's organic potential to signify and resignify within the lives of communities on the move is a key focus.

One of the unique elements of this book is that in each chapter the contributors interpret the same passage from the Christian Scriptures (New Testament) with attention to their unique social locations. Here we get an opportunity to see how the parable of the loving neighbor (often referred to as the parable of the Good Samaritan, Luke 10:25-37) is read and resonates from within a number of contexts. All but our final author, whose objectives differ slightly, interpret a passage from the Hebrew Bible (Old Testament) as well. Thus, the discussions move from theory to practice and *model* global/contextual readings. Embedded in each chapter are a series of questions that allow each reader to stop and contemplate what they have been reading and experiencing.

CONCLUDING THOUGHTS

All of the contributors represented in this volume have been im-
printed by their encounter with global theologies. We have been
shaped by these approaches, sometimes because of our engagement
with them and at other times because of our recognition that we have
not had nearly enough exposure to them. In the same ways that students will struggle with understanding and embracing marginalized
perspectives and voices, we too have struggled with the realities of
whether we can speak for the margins at all. We do not want to pretend
to speak for all who reside at the margins in totalizing ways. We can
speak to and from only the perspective we are most familiar with. So
also, we do not want to fall into the trap of homogenizing all marginal
people or speaking of them collectively; this is why our analysis has
to be as deeply personal as it is honest. This is precisely why we
gathered a number of biblically and theologically trained authors
from a variety of social locations for this book. The hope is that we
will be diligent in not essentializing any of these experiences or col-
lapsing them into the experiences of the authors. To return to the illustration of the desk mentioned at the outset of this chapter, we are
seeking to craft a space where all can read the biblical text on equal
footing and free from the constraints of the desk. In some instances,
that requires stepping down from the desk, and in other instances, it
requires liberation from under the desk. While we cannot hope in the
course of this book to eradicate the social structures represented by
the desk, we can encourage and embrace readings of the text that
promote an equality of reading from many places and social locations.
In some ways, this book is engaged in a rather artificial project; namely,
that we are categorizing the world into these sweeping geographies.
We understand that. There is a sense in which we are oversimplifying,
and there is probably as much (or more) that is missing than is
included here. This approach is not meant to minimize but to
begin conversations.

CONSIDERING THE WHOLE

- What lingering questions do you have about the ideas presented here? How might those questions be answered?

- How does your own social location interact with these questions? In other words, is there something about your own social location that is leading you to these questions?

- What are the distinctive marks of each of these reading angles?

- What seems to be the most promising aspect about contextual approaches and why?

2

LATIN AMERICAN APPROACHES

FEDERICO ALFREDO ROTH

ANY ATTEMPT TO SUMMARIZE WAYS of reading the Bible in Latin America will do well to proceed with great care. This is owing to many factors. Principally, the land mass in question includes approximately 13 percent of earth's terrain, accounts for nearly 650 million people, is composed of four subregions (North, Central, Caribbean, South), hosts twenty sovereign nations, is home to 40 percent of the world's 1.1 billion Catholics, and houses numerous ethnic groups and languages. Latin America consists of vast and immeasurably diverse places and spaces. Were we to enumerate them, they would certainly comprise tome after tome, each with flourishes of exacting detail. That Latin America hosts tremendous multicultural and multilingual diversity cannot be overstated. Neither can one exaggerate Latin America's enormous global and cultural reach. There is hardly a corner of the world that has not been marked, whether directly or through influence, by Latin America's intellectual, literary, culinary, and artistic forms of cultural production, to name a few.

For these reasons (and surely more), there is no single method or strategy for reading the Bible from a Latin American angle, or through Latin American "eyes," as it were. All eyes perceive and experience the world in unique ways, whether Latin American or otherwise. Any attempt to speak conclusively would run the risk of being imprecise at best and reductive at worst. It is vital to understand that Latin America is as culturally diverse as it is geographically expansive. And yet, while no singular claim or set of claims can do justice to the complexity of Latin American engagements with the Bible, this is not reason enough to halt the conversation before it has had a chance to begin, and before it has been given an opportunity to become profitable. There may be important things to learn by entering into a broad and knowingly imprecise discussion. These important factors notwithstanding, there are perhaps helpful generalizations—wide-ranging as they might be—to be made about this important region of the world and its contributions to biblical scholarship. What follows in the section below is a working list of those traits and trends that are most clear, most repeated, and most foundational to the multiple expressions attested in Latin American readings of the Bible. I offer them in the spirit of generosity.

In many ways, that this book should begin with a Latin American perspective is appropriate since reading the Bible in a fashion that is attuned to global perspectives is largely indebted to the pioneering efforts of South and Central American thinkers of the mid-late twentieth century. The tumultuous nature of those years gave rise to new ways of reading, interpreting, and applying the Bible. They offered new epistemological paradigms for understanding the world of the Bible, the world of the reader, and the variety of ways they overlapped and informed one another. In due time, these authors would give theological voice to a novel way for reading and engaging with Scripture. Theirs was an intrepid mode of interpretation that privileged the lived experience and suffering of communities and was unafraid of asking new sets of difficult questions. These questions were not only directed to the biblical text, but trained their attention on the contemporary world, critiquing various forms of injustice. It is in the early work of these thinkers, composed of clergy, academics, and activists, that we see the first fruits of what will later flourish into a tremendously diverse theological landscape. Indeed, any discussion of the Bible's role in Latin America does well to begin with the work of these early contributors. The new theological movement they helped create—and to which there remains a fierce commitment in various global locales—is liberation theology.

PRESENTING FEATURES AND THEMES
IN LATIN AMERICAN APPROACHES

The 1960s was a decade marked by sweeping social upheaval throughout Latin America and the world. A hallmark of the time was the sharp critique of governments and institutions seen as complicit in creating and maintaining economic inequalities responsible for expanding the divide between the so-called First and Third Worlds. As such, the era was marked by calls for an end to social, cultural, ethnic, racial, and gender injustices. The decade's attitude of suspicion was echoed in the field of theological studies, which also began to undergo its own radical shifts. This revolutionary spirit found expression in a series of significant Christian gatherings and through the publishing of important works.

Among the many pivotal events of the 1960s was the Second Vatican Council (known also as Vatican II), convened by Pope John XXIII and completed by his successor, Paul VI. Meeting in Rome from 1962 to 1965, the council undertook the task of addressing the Roman Catholic Church's relationship with the modern world through various avenues. Among them was a growing awareness of, and responsibility to redress, human suffering.[1] Another significant effect of the council's meetings

---

[1] See the papal encyclical *Mater et Magistra*, which emerged in the year prior to Vatican II (1961). Pope John XXIII, *Mater et Magistra: Christianity and Social* Progress, ed. Donald R. Campion

came about organically, as clergy members from around the world formed friendships and deepened existing bonds. In time, attendees began to share with one another their frustrations at the glacial pace of societal progress in their respective regions. They came to realize, not only that the plight of the poor was worsening, but that perhaps the church had played a role, contributing to that exploitation by both direct and passive means. The academic fields of theology and biblical studies were perhaps also complicit, in part by retreating into their respective ivory towers. Far from the suffering of the poor, academics privileged their intellectual pursuits above pressing social issues.

The suspicion and disappointment sparked by Vatican II would find sharp expression in the 1968 general conference of the Latin American episcopacy held in Medellín, Colombia. Attendees at Medellín articulated two key tenets of liberation theology. First, participants decried the suffering of the poor in Latin America as having gone well beyond interpersonal violence inflicted on individuals. Attendees denounced the plight of Latin America's downtrodden with the now-familiar expression "institutionalized violence." This phrase was used to describe the ways in which political, economic, and even religious powers conspire—intentionally and unintentionally—to create and sustain malevolent social structures that systemically imprison and disenfranchise the poor, locking them into unending cycles of economic poverty and societal humiliations. Peruvian priest and theologian Gustavo Gutiérrez, widely regarded as the father of Latin American liberation theology, reflected on the nature and scope of institutionalized violence as described by Medellín:

> In the final analysis, poverty means death: lack of food and housing, the inability to attend properly to health and education needs, the exploitation of workers, permanent unemployment, the lack of respect for

---

and Eugene K. Culhane (New York: America Press, 1961). Cf. *Populorum Progressio* (London: Catholic Truth Society, 1967). Here Pope Paul VI encouraged themes of social justice while sharply critiquing economic inequalities responsible for expanding the divide between the First and Two-Thirds World.

one's human dignity, and unjust limitations placed on personal freedom in the areas of self-expression, politics and religion. Poverty is a situation that destroys people, families, and individuals.[2]

Latin American engagement with the Bible is shaped by the experiences and questions arising from a context where inequality is endemic, and poverty is more than economic lack. To be among the poor in Latin America is to suffer destitution on a comprehensive scale. Poverty in Latin America is an attack on the gospel, a corruption of the kingdom proclaimed by Jesus. In short, it is an expression of sin. Uruguayan author Eduardo Galeano evocatively decried the resulting anguish when he wrote, "The human murder by poverty in Latin America is secret; every year, without making a sound, three Hiroshima bombs explode over communities that have become accustomed to suffering with clenched teeth."[3]

Second, Medellín turned its attention to the Bible, resisting the traditional belief that the transcendent God sits enthroned over creation as piously objective. To the contrary, the Scriptures tell of an immanent God who actively takes the side of the fragile, vulnerable, reviled, and dispossessed of the world. This is not to deny God's love for all people. Rather, Medellín affirmed that God exercises a "preferential option for the poor." As such, God is not a neutral agent who sits austerely above the created order. Rather, the immanent God disproportionately favors all who suffer injustice, and so reside on the "underside" of history. Conversely, God stands in opposition to those who create or maintain all systems of inequality.

Related to these important founding tenets, Latin American liberation theology began to formally galvanize with Gutiérrez's touchstone publishing of A Theology of Liberation (1971). Here Gutiérrez argued that the primary task of theology is not contemplative. That is, theology

---

[2]Gustavo Gutiérrez, "Introduction to the Revised Edition: Expanding the View," in A Theology of Liberation: History, Politics, and Salvation, 15th anniversary ed. (Maryknoll, NY: Orbis, 1988), xxi.
[3]Eduardo Galeano, Open Veins of Latin America: Five Centuries of the Pillage of a Continent (New York: Monthly Review Press, 1971), 5.

should not preoccupy itself with describing the nature of reality. Nor should its goal be to strengthen Christians in their faith. Neither should it organize around dogmatic theories. Much to the contrary, the central task of theology is to free the poor from situations of inhuman living conditions. All theology must therefore begin and end as an engagement with, and in, the world *before* theologizing about it.

In summary, for theology to be authentic it must resist the urge to fixate on cerebral theorizing. Theology done faithfully must be committed to the liberation of the poor. It must emanate out of experience, "from below." As the Costa Rican scholar Elsa Tamez has said, "In Latin American biblical hermeneutics, real life, corporal and sensual, lived in different concrete contexts, is the starting point for biblical analysis."[4] Latin American readings of the Bible are therefore drawn to the important theme of salvation.

Latin American readings of the Bible are deeply impacted by two of its narratives in particular. The first is the story of the Hebrew exodus from Egypt. The book of Exodus, it is argued, functions centrally as Israel's national epic, revealing God's character as one who liberates, both politically *and* spiritually. Exodus is not a bygone tale of a particular peoples' experience construed narrowly. Exodus displays God's redemptive agenda as foundational to the divine identity. God is good, loving, powerful, and committed to enacting justice (Exodus 3:7-8c). However, Exodus goes well beyond recounting the story of freedom for a singular people. The biblical tale is set in parallel to Latin America's own experience of oppression and marginalization by the economic and cultural forces of its own Egypts. As God liberated an ancient people in dignity-restoring ways, so God is committed to performing liberation for the humiliated and dispossessed of today.

The second biblical source centers on the life and ministry of Jesus. In Jesus, Latin American readings of the Bible find two important

---

[4]Elsa Tamez, "Reading the Bible Under a Sky Without Stars," in *The Bible in a World Context*, ed. Walter Dietrich and Ulrich Luz (Grand Rapids, MI: Eerdmans, 2002), 9.

points of resonance. First, Jesus inaugurates solidarity with the poor as one of God's basic priorities. Jesus shares in the hardship of oppression. Because Jesus identified intimately with oppression and sorrow, the downtrodden are invited to ally themselves to him through this shared unity. Additionally, Christ presents a model for behavior in the world. The ministry of Jesus is emblematic of one who worked as a liberator, courageously challenged the oppressive structures of his day, rehumanized the most reviled, and willingly paid the ultimate price.

It follows, then, that a Latin American understanding of salvation moves beyond a spiritual event benefiting the individual believer. Like God's earthly political liberation of Israel in the Hebrew exodus, and Jesus' bodily act of self-sacrifice, full freedom can only be realized concretely, communally, and intrahistorically. God's saving agenda is comprehensive, eradicating social, political, economic, institutional, and societal structures that seek to disempower entire communities. The experience of salvation also carries cognitive qualities as the newly liberated throw off the effects of inner servitude as well. Freedom means more than liberation *from* slavery. To be free means charting one's own destiny. In short, to be saved is to be free—here and now—in both tangible and psychological ways. Freedom will mean truly worshiping God, who can only be encountered in a setting of liberation.[5]

A third feature of Latin American readings of the Bible is awareness. This requires that subject groups first come to recognize the forces that oppress them. To this end, Paulo Freire, a Brazilian educator and author, argues that an essential aspect of achieving liberation is conscientization, a term that means "making aware."[6] Here the subjected group recognizes the structures by which they are dehumanized and in which they are confined. But simply recognizing the shape and

---

[5]Gustavo Gutiérrez, *The God of Life* (Maryknoll, NY: Orbis Books, 1989), 4.
[6]Paulo Freire, *Pedagogy of the Oppressed*, trans. Myra Bergman Ramos (New York: Herder and Herder, 1970).

scope of urgent problems is not enough. Once cognizant of their plight, the afflicted must then act. Like God, Latin Americans are to serve as architects of liberation in their own right, *participating* in the building of more just societies by deploying strategies of resistance and survival. This task may take many forms. Whether this cooperation entails resisting ideologies in subtle ways or through tangible political efforts at community organizing and demonstrating, liberation must take shape as *lucha* (struggle/fight) against all forms of alienation and exclusion. Whatever the medium, individuals and communities are called to contribute. It is vitally important that the act of commitment, or praxis, comes before all else. Once this first act has taken shape, reflection on praxis, that is, theologizing, may follow. As Gutiérrez states, "It is not enough to say that love of God is inseparable from the love of one's neighbor. It must be added that love for God is unavoidably expressed *through* love of one's neighbor."[7]

With a backdrop in place, we are poised to read specific scriptural passages. What does a uniquely Latin American perspective contribute to a careful analysis of the biblical text? What do Latin American eyes see that other eyes cannot? An exposition of Luke 10:25-37 and Deuteronomy 24:17-22 will help us explore these questions and arrive at some helpful insights.

STOP AND THINK

- What are some ways in which institutionalized violence remains a challenge to be addressed? How have you experienced institutionalized violence and/or its effects?

- Consider the idea of God's "preferential option for the poor." In what ways is it a helpful way of thinking about God? In what ways does it pose new challenges to thinking about God?

---

[7]Gutiérrez, *Theology of Liberation*, 114-15.

- In what ways does the church privilege theologizing be-fore committed action (praxis)?

- The exodus and life of Jesus are important connecting points for Latin American readings of the Bible. Can you think of other biblical stories in which the ideas of liberation and solidarity are foregrounded?

READING TEXTS

The Parable of the Loving Neighbor (Luke 10:25-37)

The parable of the loving neighbor, commonly but unhelpfully called the "Good Samaritan" (Luke 10:25-37),[8] is introduced by a travel narrative in which Jesus sends envoys in thirty-five pairs to locations he intends to visit. Their return is cause for great celebration as they report a successful campaign of healing the sick and proclaiming the kingdom of God. Shortly thereafter, Jesus is challenged by a lawyer's question: "What must I do to inherit eternal life?"

Jesus meets his inquiry with another question in rebuttal. "What is written in the law? What do you read there?" (Luke 10:26). The lawyer answers piously, quoting Deuteronomy and Leviticus in combination, "You shall love the Lord your God with all your heart and with all your soul and with all your strength and with all your mind and your neighbor as yourself" (Luke 10:27; see also Deuteronomy 6:5; Leviticus 19:18). Pleased with the answer, Jesus instructs him to "do this, and you will live" (Luke 10:28). The self, we learn through the lawyer's admission, is not partitioned into discrete sectors. Rather, love of God, neighbor, and self are inextricably linked to one another, forming a whole. Love for God is all-encompassing, working its way in and through multiple dimensions of human self-expression. Love for God lays claim to all aspects of the

---

[8]This inaccuracy is owing to the fact that nowhere is the Samaritan called "good." The use of "good" also implies that this Samaritan is uniquely virtuous as compared to his wicked compatriots.

human experience. Community and human selfhood work in unison, mirroring love of God. What is more, love is not one's reserved and restricted, tight-fisted possession. Nor is the authenticity of love judged in sheer affection for God and God alone. To the contrary, authentic love is marked by its willingness to reach for the other. Love for one's self and love for one's neighbor go hand in glove. Eternal life, then, recalling the first question ("What must I do to inherit eternal life?"), is not that which can be *received*. Eternal life must be *exercised* ("do this") through love, in daily, ongoing, and comprehensive ways. In short, eternal life is demystified. It is not the culmination of a life already lived. One may indeed live in an "eternal" fashion by behaving in ordinary ways.

Having arrived at his answer, which depicts love as lavish, supremely generous, and eminently ordinary, the lawyer scrutinizes his own words for clarification. He persists, "And who is my neighbor?" (Luke 10:29). We might rephrase his question as, "To whom must I extend this wide-ranging care?" Or perhaps better yet, "Who, like God, is worthy of such radical love?" Jesus replies with the famous parable:

> "A man was going down from Jerusalem to Jericho, and fell into the hands of robbers, who stripped him, beat him, and went away, leaving him half dead. Now by chance a priest was going down that road; and when he saw him, he passed by on the other side. So likewise a Levite, when he came to the place and saw him, passed by on the other side. But a Samaritan while traveling came near him; and when he saw him, he was moved with pity. He went to him and bandaged his wounds, having poured oil and wine on them. Then he put him on his own animal, brought him to an inn, and took care of him. The next day he took out two denarii, gave them to the innkeeper, and said, 'Take care of him; and when I come back, I will repay you whatever more you spend.' Which of these three, do you think, was a neighbor to the man who fell into the hands of the robbers?" He said, "The one who showed him mercy." Jesus said to him, "Go and do likewise."

The scene of the parable is set in the rugged hills and valleys winding from the heights of Jerusalem, down a narrow path leading to Jericho in the low country called the Jordan River Valley. In total, the path's distance approximates fifteen to seventeen miles (approx. 24–27 km) and drops some three thousand feet. Even today, visitors to the region regularly cite the rather remote and precarious nature of the trail. Steep screes and vertical drops imperil the careless wanderer on their descent to the valley floor below. The topography leaves few options for ingress or egress, making it all the more dangerous for those who dare travel alone.

The assault on the anonymous man happens swiftly. He is robbed (stripped), beaten, and left exposed on the path (Luke 10:30). The opening phrase of Luke 10:31, "Now by chance," is optimistic in its tone. The natural expectation is that the first to appear, the priest, will lend aid. And yet, the arrival of the cleric is no solution. Whatever hope he embodies is dashed in a moment. The horror of the scene is magnified by the constraints of the path itself. The narrow way would have likely meant the priest must carefully step over the wounded man, taking in the full gruesomeness of his injuries.

From the specific description of the priest, the story broadens to recount the arrival of a lay member of the priestly tribe, a Levite (Luke 10:32). Having also seen and stepped over, the Levite moves on. The men are joined, perhaps, in their mutual desire to remain ceremonially clean, given that contact with a dead man would result in ritual impurity (see Leviticus 21:1-3; Numbers 5:2; 19:11-13; cf. Ezekiel 44: 25-27). In Luke 10:33, we arrive at a disjunctive clause introduced by the Greek *de* ("but"). This opening word not only emphasizes that at long last a rescuer has arrived on scene; it may also signal the biblical author's recognition that the saving figure—a Samaritan—is of an unexpected and lowly social profile.

Historical Background: Samaritans

In the first century CE, Samaritans were a conservative northern sect of Judaism. Their background is not wholly known. They were perhaps descended from exiled immigrants at the hands of Assyrian conquerors, or the products of intermarriage with the remnant population following the destruction of northern Israel in 722 BCE.

Whatever their precise origin, there is some consensus that by the time of Jesus they venerated their own Pentateuch (the first five books of the Hebrew Bible), kept strict dietary laws, and worshiped atop Mount Gerizim (Deuteronomy 11:29; 27:12) as opposed to in Jerusalem. Their kinsmen to the south harbored, therefore, a deep enmity and animosity toward them. This hostility is clearly detected in other New Testament passages where Samaritans are either denigrated and defamed (John 8:48) or understood to be isolated from their southern brethren (John 4:9).

Against the prestigious title of priest and the vaunted pedigree of the Levite—both representing indisputable insiders—the Samaritan embodies the strangeness and otherness of the enemy outsider (see above).

The Samaritan traveler also sees. Unlike his forerunners, only he is moved to act. We read twice that he moves toward him ("came near him," Luke 10:33, and "went to him," Luke 10:34), applying antiseptics and bandaging his wounds on site. The gravity of the injuries is highlighted by the fact that the injured man cannot walk but must be transported atop the animal. The Samaritan's travel itinerary—we might assume—is abandoned or postponed as he delivers the injured man to safety. Having looked after him for the remainder of the day, and having enlisted the help of the innkeeper, the Samaritan promises to cover additional expenses on his return with a proverbial blank check—an act of overabundant generosity with potentially damaging economic ramifications. The Samaritan meets and exceeds hospitality rites. Having finished the tale, Jesus again questions the lawyer.

"Which of these three, do you think, was a neighbor to the man who fell into the hands of the robbers?" The answer says nothing of the Samaritan's cultural background. Rather, it centers on his *actions*. "The one who *showed* him mercy." Having answered rightly, all that is left is activity. Jesus instructs, "Go and do likewise" (Luke 10:37).

The parable of the loving neighbor has much to teach its hearers and readers. It stretches back to the accompanying question: "And who is my neighbor?" (Luke 10:29). Jesus senses in the question, posed from a member of the elite, a certain reticence, perhaps an unwillingness to recognize the correspondence between love for God and love for neighbor in the keeping of the law. The fact that the priest and Levite are also elites carries rhetorical effect. Status and prestige (or the lack thereof) are not guarantors for law keeping. Perhaps the desires of the priest and Levite to maintain purity made them impure. Paradoxically, there are times when admonitions to act in keeping with the law result in violations of it. Mercy, we learn, comes without qualifications of any type. The lawyer's question, not unlike the sidestepping of the injured man, sought to parse the meaning of love. Rather than giving love freely and generously, the very utterance of the question signals the lawyer's proclivity to also "step over" the wounded man.

It is typical to read this parable as a story of simple moralizing. To this end, one can readily recognize that Jesus reframes the question. The lawyer's question, not unlike the sidestepping of the injured man, seeks to parse love. The rhetorical turn is an effective one. Jesus offers an answer to a question that was not asked, but that nevertheless serves as an answer in its own right, while also going beyond the shortsightedness of the original question itself. Like the Samaritan, who lavishes care and attention, so also the answer is richer, more profound than the simplicity of the question. The teaching is as follows: Don't strain to distinguish the neighbor in your midst, the insiders from the outsiders. One must put aside social status and prestige to bind the broken. Strive to *become* the loving neighbor.

Emulate him, putting aside meaningless issues of status. All can and must behave in neighborly ways. Don't relate to the world in such a manner that you rest at its center. Rather, like the Samaritan, practice bridging the distance by moving away from self and *toward* the other in ways that promote healing and restoration.

Added to this, we do well to recall that the lawyer's initial question centered on eternal life. If eternal life can be secured by holistic love of God *and* neighborliness, then we now see the extent of this neighborliness. Neither religious nor hereditary status will result in eternal life. Indeed, love of God is bankrupt if it does not also mean exercising love for neighbor. At its core, this message is worthy of merit. Indeed, even the casual reader can recognize the importance of looking beyond the self when the neighbor is imperiled. And yet, while a Latin American reading will agree with many of the foregoing conclusions, it will probe the parable in new ways, resulting in unexpected outcomes.

A Latin American **vista.** Many Latin Americans will resonate with the parable of the loving neighbor because it is, in some ways, a tale of migration, and migration has come to define the lives of many Latin Americans. We recall that the Samaritan engages the injured man "while traveling" (Luke 10:33). It cannot be overemphasized that the Samaritan, for reasons already identified, would have represented an unauthorized individual, descended from those of an alien ethnic population. This vulnerability is heightened by the fact that the story is set far from his home (the north), in a place of implicit and explicit hostility; the place bracketed between the quintessential Jewish cities of Jerusalem and Jericho (the south). As an alien in an alien territory, the Samaritan suffers an "un/under-documented" status as unauthorized and "illegal" among southerners, not unlike today's Latin American border crossers and boundary breakers. Like them, the Samaritan is navigating his own experiences of dislocation and deauthorization. The kindness he exhibits is heightened by his fragile sociopolitical status and threats to his own well-being. In Jesus' story it is the alienated one who, through his own agency and kindness, breathes hope to those in positions of power and privilege. Only he is well-placed to bring an end to the cycle of dehumanization.

As the source of benevolence and survival, this Latin American reading recognizes that compassion cannot be circumscribed by boundaries, borders, or barriers. Jesus teaches that those who transgress borders (geographical and otherwise), inhabiting the most vulnerable positions, are poised to recognize the broken among them and act on their behalf. They are the embodiment of the gospel, which itself represents an inbreaking of God into history. We err if we interpret the aim of the parable as somehow going beyond identity. The Samaritan does not transcend his low social position. Indeed, it *is* his low social position and identity that give him the needed eyes to see the humanity in another wounded figure. The Samaritan (and those who share in his lowly status) alone can break the ongoing sequence of estrangement. It is those who have themselves been alienated that are in the best positions to recognize and defeat alienation from within. The most forgotten, most vulnerable, most objectionable, are the most well-placed to reach for their enemy, bringing an end to the circuits of violence, whether physical or psychological. What is more, by making the Samaritan into the hero, Jesus scandalizes his audience. Locating human kindness, dignity, and agency in the figure of the most despised exposes stereotyping practices as meritless. For Latin American readers, this story forms a counterweight to the racist tropes in our own day that would disfigure their people as simple, backward, lazy, lecherous, and dangerous.

Perhaps also, a Latin American reading will alert the Bible reader to another dimension of identity's complex nature. It is typical to note a certain irony in the parable—namely, that those who possess access to power (priest and Levite), and are most celebrated for that power, can be the least capable of deploying it toward loving ends. The privilege of pedigree and social status can serve as obstacles blocking the path to genuine care. But a Latin American reading will go further, straining to exercise compassion on the would-be villains by unearthing another injurious dimension in the story. That is, the fallen man is not the only figure that suffers loss. The reticence of the priest and Levite to render aid is itself a costly one. For in refusing to help the wounded man, another wound is created. Through their negligence, the priest and Levite suffer their own disfigurement. As they become less apt to recognize the human in their midst, so their own humanity is threatened and maligned. Their inaction amounts to a forfeiture of their own humanity. As Latin American liberation theologians have taught, injustice is not unidirectional. Rather, it savages oppressed and oppressor alike. The duo loses out on more than an opportunity to help the wounded man. Their careful stepping over and around betrays a kind of self-care. Violence that is institutionalized can assault even its main actors. The priest and Levite are victimized by the assumptions and presumptions of their own making. They are victims of their own inaction, and so leave a part of themselves on the path. The parable is not about a single wounded man, but three.

Finally, Latin American eyes will perhaps recognize that kindness is exercised in community, by the eclectic tandem of the Samaritan outsider *and* the innkeeper insider, who together orchestrate the care and survival of the traveler. This cooperative element suggests two things. First, we learn that justice making is a collective endeavor uniting marginal *and* central figures in a common purpose. The mutual concern for the injured man serves to bridge social and economic divisions, which might otherwise keep these two men apart, and brings them into community with one another. Perhaps embedded here is the lesson that care for the downtrodden entails a partnership with the potential to join all people in ways that cut across sociopolitical lines. The preferential option can be executed by God and also by the community of God. Second, the tale serves as a warning of sorts, not simply to resist the behaviors of the priest and Levite, but to ward against creating a new enemy. Rather than refashioning alienation by vilifying the priest and Levite, as their society has done to the Samaritan, the partnership of the Samaritan and innkeeper breathes hope for the futures of the privileged as well. The salvation/liberation of the priest and Levite are also in view. Perhaps with time they too will join future "innkeepers" in ways that save and restore life wherever and whenever it is imperiled.

Memory and Justice: Deuteronomy 24:17-22

A particularly compelling passage comes in the book of Deuteronomy, which recalls the stories of Israel's wilderness wanderings and the receiving of the law, God's statutes for the building of a healthy society. Having just survived the exodus from Egypt and at last traveling to the edge of the Promised Land, Israel gathers for the second of Moses' three addresses (Deuteronomy 5–28). It is typical to divide these chapters into two parts. Deuteronomy 5–11 announce the formal giving of the law. Here one finds the Decalogue (commonly called the Ten Commandments), directives on conquest wars, and stark warnings about the need for obedience. Deuteronomy 12–28 move the discussion to life's more practical matters. Here one finds guidelines legislating idolatrous places of worship, dietary customs, debt remission, slave release, yearly festivals, judicial procedures, the priesthood, refuge cities, holy war, and both family and civic duties.

In Deuteronomy 24:17-22, one such set of community obligations centers on the responsibilities shared by all landowning males. The passage reads as follows:

> You shall not deprive a resident alien or an orphan of justice; you shall not take a widow's garment in pledge. Remember that you were a slave in Egypt and the LORD your God redeemed you from there; therefore I command you to do this. When you reap your harvest in your field and forget a sheaf in the field, you shall not go back to get it; it shall be left for the alien, the orphan, and the widow, so that the LORD your God may bless you in all your undertakings. When you beat your olive trees, do not strip what is left; it shall be for the alien, the orphan, and the widow. When

you gather the grapes of your vineyard, do not glean what is left; it shall
be for the alien, the orphan, and the widow. Remember that you were a
slave in the land of Egypt; therefore I am commanding you to do this.

Moses' directive is compelling, largely because it appeals to Israel's
memory of the exodus. Here, the antidote to poverty is remembrance.
The fact that Deuteronomy 24:18 and 22 bookend the passage attests
to this focus. The Israelites are to recall their own national status as
marked by a parallel defenselessness. They must recall their dependence on God, who was ultimately responsible for leading them into
the freedom they now enjoy. The "therefore" in verse 18 provides the
rationale for the practical instructions that follow. Because God has
redeemed, so now the people must work in redemptive ways. The
freedom they now enjoy bears a circular quality. The redeemed must
function in redemptive ways.

The climactic saving deed accomplished by God in the exodus is to
be reimagined in the events of daily Israelite agricultural life. Deuteronomy 24:19-21 each begin with the temporal "when," implying
routine tasks undertaken on a regular schedule. The instructions are
eminently practical. First, the forgotten bundles must be left behind
(Deuteronomy 24:19). The harvesting of olive trees, which was done
by using long poles to strike branches, must not involve horizontal
use of that tool to strip olives that remain (Deuteronomy 24:20). Presumably, only ripe olives would fall to the ground when branches
were struck. Lastly, the final directive warns against over-harvesting
grapes. As with harvesting the olive orchard, perhaps leaving un-
ripened grapes on the vine is in view.

In its conclusion, the passage returns to the crucial logic supporting
this call for kindness (Deuteronomy 24:18). Deuteronomy 24:22 reads,
"Remember that you were a slave in the land of Egypt; therefore I am
commanding you to do this." By twice echoing the exodus story,
Deuteronomy 24:22 cements the critical reasoning. The care of God
exhibited in Egypt, one might say, is replayed again and again as those

who benefit from the power of land ownership and its riches extend grace and mercy to those with limited power. To behave kindly is to simulate the work of God's own kindness.

By showing compassion to the weak, Israel not only revitalizes its memory of national liberation, but it defuses the tendency to exercise oppressive Pharaoh-like negligence. Failure to perform in such life-giving ways is to duplicate Egypt's oppression. Will Israel, now gazing at the Promised Land in the distance, form a society that protects and dignifies its most impoverished? Will Israel exercise God's saving power? Or will Israel, like Egypt, devise new ways to exploit the already exploited?

A Latin American **vista.** As with the parable of the loving neighbor, a Latin American reading of this passage seeks to add to the preceding by unearthing additional discoveries. For one, the precise nature of the suffering experienced by the alien, orphan, and widow will be foregrounded in an attempt to fully appreciate their plight. While all experienced unique forms of alienation in ancient Israelite society, they were imperiled in at least four shared ways. First, daily survival was always in question given that, as an agricultural society, Israel was structured and organized around the nuclear and extended family system. To be widowed, orphaned, or to live as an alien was—by definition—to experience severely weakened or nonexistent bonds to family. Second, long-term survival was also in jeopardy given that each member of the triad is distanced from inheritance rights, and thus, the wealth and produce that can only come through land rights. Third, each was disadvantaged in the legal setting, where only land-owning males might use power, wealth, and status to sway court rulings in their favor (see Deuteronomy 1:16-18; Ruth 4). Finally, aliens, orphans, and widows might also suffer the unrelenting psycho-logical blows of incessant social stigma born of a narrow, and thus restrictive, brand of theology. This thinking, commonly called retrib-utive theology, taught that God blessed and punished according to one's behavior. Riches and blessing were the natural outcomes of an obedient life. So also, poverty and affliction were the product of rebellious living. And so it was that the alien, orphan, and widow not only suffered the daily lack of basic necessities, the uncertainties about their long-term survival, and diminished legal rights, but they also endured a quiet humiliation in the eyes of those who considered their lot as God's punishment for wickedness.

A Latin American reader might linger here, contemplating the manifold experience of suffering faced by the trio as emblematic of a shared experience. Latin American readers will perhaps resonate with the legacy of violence in antiquity as manifested in modern institutionalized forms resulting in socioeconomic imbalances *still* operative in their own communities. They will readily recognize the story of the ancient alien, orphan, and widow as one marked by shortage and peril. Such scarcity may be measured as lacking material goods necessary for daily survival. Perhaps it may be measured as a dearth of access to adequate education, quality healthcare, political representation, or as is often the case, all of these factors simultaneously. Or even still, we might consider their suffering more obliquely as an unceasing lack of social status, dignity, and respect.

As a once-undocumented immigrant to the United States, I resonate with the experiences of the alien, orphan, and widow, if in my own small way. While I have been fortunate never to suffer from lack of basic resources, I am not unfamiliar with the psychological disjointedness faced by fellow immigrants. Indeed, from time to time an experience in daily life will conjure feelings of alienation and estrangement. Some I anticipate, some catch me wholly unawares. One such instance comes to mind from my early years as an academic. During a faculty meeting, a colleague began to share excitement at having just received their green card, guaranteeing them the right to work and remain in the United States. They were pleased to share that the matter had not been very difficult to complete. The university had paid an immigration lawyer to "expedite" the process, which, in a matter of months, had secured their legal status. Much to my surprise, the card was then produced and offered up for examination. We were to appreciate its high-tech properties, which included a hologram watermark. I was, of course, happy for my colleague and the milestone represented in the act of receiving this important form of documentation. And yet, as the card was passed from one to another, I could not help but feel a growing mixture of sadness and grief come over me.

The item in question—*this particular item*—perhaps unlike any other item, carried a sacred symbolism. Not that America had been any kind of religious haven or imbued with any more religious significance than my native Uruguay. But rather, my angst was sourced in the near-callous way in which the card was being so nonchalantly displayed as an object of curiosity to be handled and ogled. When it finally came to me, I passed it quickly down the line, making the conscious choice to glance at it briefly but respectfully. For my family, that strip of plastic was a symbol fraught with tremendous meaning. On the one hand, it represented the uncertainties and vulnerabilities of living an unauthorized existence in a distant land. The years spent yearning for it, and its absence in our lives, was a source of untold pain and uncertainty. And yet it was simultaneously an object imbued with hope and promise. Aspiring to possess such a thing was, for my parents, an enterprise worthy of overturning and rewriting the narrative life of an entire family and recharting its course irrevocably. For us, residency (and later citizenship) came at a steep price given the geographical and emotional distance immigration would place between my nuclear and extended family. The price of that plastic was measured in severed relationships. To possess such an object would mean leaving behind aunts, uncles, cousins, and our only living grandparent. While it is true that securing residency did not bring an end to our experiences of dislocation, it is equally true that having official paperwork brought, at long last, some psychological relief.

Second, Latin American readers will perhaps notice how the Deuteronomy regulations aim to address, if in an implicit way, the psychological well-being of the alien, orphan, and widow. The agricultural instructions address the physical needs of the triad, but they also resist the dehumanizing effects of poverty faced by the group, particularly that of isolation brought about by joblessness. In each instance, the alien, orphan, and widow are not merely passive recipients of charity. The landowner provides ready produce, but nothing more. The means for self-preservation belong to the poor. When one follows in the path of grain collectors, olive gatherers, and vineyard harvesters, they labor for their own survival. In this way, the poor are given the resources by which they provide for their own needs. What is more, the dignity and value of these groups is maintained by virtue of the important role (secondary harvesters) they now embody as members of the community. Thus, while the word is never used, this is undoubtedly a salvation passage insofar as those who are most vulnerable experience a comprehensive rescue from servitude and poverty, whether material or psychological.

Finally, it will not be lost on the Latin American reader that Israel is here given the opportunity to exercise a "preferential option" for the poor as they re-create and mirror the faithfulness shown to them by God. In this passage, awareness is not enough. The circuit is complete *only* when mindfulness has turned to action. The passage is not content to merely recognize the sorrows and sinfulness of injustice. Anticipating the spirit of Latin American Bible reading, recognition must move to *active participation*.

REFLECTING ON THE TEXTS

- Where do you suppose the boundaries of neighborliness are drawn in today's day and age? What does a Latin American reading teach us about one's responsibility toward vulnerable groups?

- In what ways do we "step over" wounded persons and groups? In what ways can we "step toward" them?

- Which groups in modern society share in the suffering of the alien, orphan, and widow?

- Consider the instructions set forth in Deuteronomy 24:17-22. What are some examples of tangible actions that can be undertaken to reverse the suffering of disempowered populations in today's world?

CONCLUDING THOUGHTS

Latin American readings of the Bible offer uniquely sensitive engagements with Scripture. Underappreciated biblical characters that live at the margins of power, whether social, economic, or otherwise, resonate with Latin American experiences and so provide avenues for fresh engagement with the Bible. This way of understanding privileges the life of the interpreter as vital for reaching conclusions. Against spiritualized interpretations that would make abstract the narratives of Scripture, Latin American readings breathe new life into familiar stories. The Bible is not an inert object or set of antiquated dictums. Rather, foundational is the belief that Scripture offers a pattern for God's interventionism in the world. There is a certain continuity existing between ancient and modern settings. Because God acted to bring about sociopolitical salvation and justice for Israel, so God remains committed to that same saving agenda today. Or, as Stephen J. Binz so aptly expresses the matter:

> The God of the exodus continues to intervene. God rescues us in desperate moments and orients us toward new understandings and new goals. Within our lives we will encounter new Pharaohs and new Egypts, people and situations that enslave and destroy life. We will also discover new Moses figures, new deserts, new Sinais and new promised lands. We will find people and experiences that reveal good, dangerous places of divine interaction, situations that liberate us and renew our life. Like the

Israelites, we fear the unknown, though in accordance with God's initiative, we leave behind safety and march forward. The experience of the
exodus makes us capable of retaining confidence, to know that God,
who has been faithful in the past, will be by our side in the journey and
will take us to the fullness of life (my translation).[9]

Reading through Latin American eyes is to see how the God of the
Bible comes alive in our world to work in life-giving and liberating ways.

CONSIDERING THE WHOLE

- What are some ways that Latin American readings of the
  Bible contribute to your understanding of Scripture? In
  what ways does this way of reading pose new questions or
  challenges? What are they?

- How has this mode for reading alerted you to your own
  social location and its influence on your reading of the
  Bible? How do you suspect it has helped you to see and
  understand in new ways?

SUGGESTIONS FOR FURTHER READING

Brown, Robert McAfee. *Unexpected News: Reading the Bible with Third World Eyes.*
Louisville, KY: Westminster Press, 1984.

Croatto, J. Severino. *Exodus: A Hermeneutics of Freedom.* Maryknoll, NY: Orbis Books, 1978.

Ferm, Deane William. *Third World Liberation Theologies: An Introductory Survey.*
Eugene, OR: Wipf & Stock, 1986.

González, Justo L. *Mañana: Christian Theology from a Hispanic Perspective.* Nashville:
Abingdon, 1990.

Isasi-Díaz, Ada María. *Mujerista Theology: A Theology for the Twenty-First Century.*
Maryknoll, NY: Orbis Books, 1996.

---

[9]Stephen J. Binz, *El Dios de la Libertad y de la Vida: Un Comentario sobre el libro del Exodo*, trans.
Colette Joly Dees (Collegeville, MN: The Order of St. Benedict, 1995), 11.

3

AFRICAN APPROACHES

ALICE YAFEH-DEIGH

THERE IS AN INFLUX OF VOICES in African biblical scholarship from sub-Saharan social locations. These voices are part of the current surge in new interpretive paradigms in biblical studies as a whole. These new approaches have significantly broadened the scope of biblical analysis to include interpreters' views from many social locations. Many of these new approaches focus on biblical contextual hermeneutics that privilege lived and embodied experiences of both ancient and modern readers. I use the term *Africa* in this chapter not as a monolithic, homogenous entity. The African continent as a whole comprises fifty-four countries. Of the fifty-four countries, forty-eight of them constitute what is known as sub-Saharan Africa.[1] The fifty-four countries are highly diverse socially, culturally, religiously, ethnically, and linguistically. It is absolutely a misnomer to refer to Africa

---

[1]There are two cultural groups in Africa: North Africa (geographically located north of the Sahara Desert) and sub-Saharan Africa (located south of the Sahara Desert). Historically, North Africa (Morocco, Algeria, Tunisia, Libya, and Egypt) has had strong ties to and affinity with the Middle East. North African countries are predominantly Arab countries. This socio-religious location explains why these countries are easily grouped with the Middle East. Also, North Africa is comparatively more developed than sub-Saharan Africa. Skin complexion is an added factor. Physically, North Africans are of generally lighter skin complexion.

as if it were a single country. However, there exist some commonalities among the diverse sub-Saharan regions. The quintessential similarity is the shared collective memory of the colonial past and the cultural legacies of colonialism in the postcolonial present. Other commonalities are shared cultural heritage, patriarchal structures, and social characteristics. As a result of these commonalities, African biblical scholars maintain that it is possible to use the same interpretive frameworks/perspectives to address the multidimensional sociocultural groups in the continent because the frameworks will, by necessity, be differently contextualized across the continent.[2]

African biblical scholarship's approaches equally acknowledge that widely divergent interpretive results may be obtained even when the same methodological standards are used because unique ideologies are present in all interpretive processes. Take the practice of translation as a case in point. Why do we have multiple different translations of the Bible in English? It is because translators often have to make a range of interpretive judgment calls whenever textual meaning is complicated, which it almost always is. Since complex words usually have a broad semantic range, translators or commentators are obliged to make choices within that semantic range; thus, we have different translations that may communicate equally plausible and legitimate readings. In the same manner, interpreters are often compelled to make contextual choices in their understanding of the language of a story or text. The variety of interpretations offered should not be viewed as contradictory but should be considered as resting within a "complementary range of meanings."[3]

The consensus among African biblical scholars, continental and diasporic[4] alike, is that the African context and African lived realities

---

[2]The adjective *African* is used here to refer to the forty-eight countries comprising sub-Saharan Africa.

[3]Brian Blount, *Cultural Interpretation: Reorienting New Testament Criticism* (Minneapolis: Fortress, 1995), 176.

[4]By African diasporic scholars, I mean African scholars who live outside of Africa. I use it to refer explicitly to Africans who migrated voluntarily to the United States and Europe. In

serve as a starting point and the primary subject of biblical interpretation. Therefore, African biblical scholarship categorically "refuses to deal with the Bible simply as an ancient text and demands that it be engaged to deal with present concerns, addressing issues that resonate with African (and world) realities."[5] As Gerald West aptly puts it, "Interpreting the biblical text is never, in African biblical hermeneutics, an end in itself. Biblical interpretation is always about changing the African context. This is what links ordinary African biblical interpretation and African biblical scholarship, a common commitment to 'read' the Bible for personal and societal transformation."[6] The work of the African biblical scholar shows a strong commitment to liberation and social transformation. Thus, interpreters from African social locations, in their interaction with the Bible in many different ways, foreground themselves as real flesh-and-blood readers, variously situated in front of the text. The interpretive priority is always given to real flesh-and-blood readers' role and is consciously rooted in their everyday life; hence, African biblical scholarship's engagement with the Bible is reader-oriented and praxis-oriented. It makes explicit the social location within which it is theorizing and interpreting; therefore, its conclusions are unavoidably subjective. The interpreter is an interested, not a disinterested or neutral, observer.

PRESENTING FEATURES AND THEMES IN AFRICAN APPROACHES

African biblical scholarship has adopted a wide variety of investigative tools forged not out of the world of scholarship alone, but out of a range of political, social, spiritual, and cultural contexts. It finds its focus in the distinct social, cultural, contextual, and linguistic

---

different contexts, the term refers to both Africans who moved freely and those who were forcefully brought to North America through the transatlantic slave trade.

[5]Andrew Mbuvi, "African Biblical Studies: An Introduction to an Emerging Discipline," *Currents in Biblical Research* 15 (2017), 154.

[6]Gerald West, "Biblical Hermeneutics in Africa," in *African Theology on the Way*, ed. D. B. Stinton, International Study Guide 46 (London: SPCK, 2010), 22-23.

variables that shape and influence its particular reading of the biblical texts. While these emphases are by no means comprehensive, they provide a foundation for exploring several approaches within African biblical scholarship.[7]

I will highlight here some of the critical approaches to African biblical scholarship.[8] Between the 1950s and 1980s, following Africa's political independence, African theologians pushed for a hermeneutic of rehabilitation/resonance that sought to redeem African Christian identity from past stigmas by demonstrating resonances between African religious realities and the Bible.[9] The similarities between the stories, religious practices, and institutions of the Bible and African cultures make the Bible much more relevant and pertinent to African cultural experiences. After the hermeneutic of rehabilitation/resonance arose, inculturation/cultural hermeneutics went beyond locating parallels between the biblical text and the African context. Cultural hermeneutics drives the need to analyze biblical interpretations disseminated by African churches and treat such analyses and African realities as viable starting points for theology.[10] Thus, the African context and "the questions that arise therefrom"[11] became an essential subject of biblical interpretation. Between the 1960s and 1980s, and originating as a reaction against apartheid, liberationist readings often drifted toward Moses or Micah.[12] While both extol the

---

[7]For a detailed summary of contemporary scholarship on sub-Saharan African contextual hermeneutics, see Mbuvi, "African Biblical Studies."

[8]Even though Mbuvi's article is not meant to be a comprehensive review of all the methods, he has effectively and concisely summarized the main hermeneutical approaches used in African biblical hermeneutics. I am indebted to him for the summary of the methodologies presented here.

[9]Mbuvi, "African Biblical Studies," 160; E. Bolaji Idowu, *Olodumare: God in Yoruba Belief* (London: Longmans, 1962); John S. Mbiti, *Concepts of God in Africa* (London: SPCK), 1970.

[10]Mbuvi, "African Biblical Studies," 161; Justin Ukpong, "Rereading the Bible with African Eyes: Inculturation and Hermeneutics," *JTSA* 91 (1995): 3-14. Cf. Justin S. Ukpong, "Bible Reading with a Community of Ordinary Readers," in *Interpreting the New Testament in Africa*, ed. Mary N. Getui, Tinyiko Maluleke, and Justin S. Ukpong (Nairobi: Acton, 2001), 188-212.

[11]Ukpong, "Rereading the Bible with African Eyes," 4.

[12]Mbuvi, "African Biblical Studies," 162; Itumeleng J. Mosala, *Biblical Hermeneutics and Black Theology in South Africa* (Grand Rapids, MI: Eerdmans, 1989); Gerald West, *Reading Otherwise:*

liberationist enterprise, readings of the latter notably emphasize that
the "black liberation struggle . . . is the *bona fide* entrance into a
genuine African biblical hermeneutics."[13] Liberationist readings stress
"the economic and the political dimensions of African life,"[14] with race
and class being its critical categories.

African feminist/womanist theology,[15] which has remained
prominent since the 1980s, centralizes gender as an entry into a
more multidimensional analysis of the Bible, patriarchal cultural
heritage, and colonial legacies.[16] For example, in responding to African inculturation theology's patriarchal and androcentric orien-
tation, Musimbi Kanyoro notes that "inculturation is not sufficient
unless the cultures we reclaim are analyzed and are deemed worthy

---

Socially Engaged Biblical Scholars Reading with Their Local Communities, Semeia, 62 (Atlanta:
Society of Biblical Literature), 2007.

[13]Mbuvi, "African Biblical Studies," 162.

[14]West, *Reading Otherwise*, 4.

[15]Although the noun *feminism* assumes many contextual definitions, it is broadly construed as
a framework for promoting the full humanity and dignity of all women. Since the term was
used historically to prioritize White Euro-American women's concerns, women of color have
used adjectives to qualify the noun or have coined various alternatives to address women of
color's specific oppression and lived experiences. African American women adopted Alice
Walker's alternative term *womanist* to deal with their actual experiences, particularly regarding
how race and class dynamics intersect with gender. For African scholars who do feminist
hermeneutics, see Mbuvi, "African Biblical Studies," 161; Mercy Amber Oduyoye, *Daughters of
Anowa: African Women and Patriarchy* (Maryknoll, NY: Orbis, 1995). Cf. Oduyoye, *Hearing
and Knowing: Theological Reflections on Christianity in Africa* (Maryknoll, NY: Orbis, 2001);
Madopoane Masenya, "African Womanist Hermeneutics: A Suppressed Voice from South
Africa Speaks," *Journal of Feminist Studies* 11 (1995): 149-55; *How Worthy Is the Woman of Worth?
Rereading Proverbs 31:10–31 in African South Africa* (New York: Peter Lang), 2004; Musa Dube,
Postcolonial Feminist Interpretation of the Bible (St. Louis: Chalice, 2000); "Rereading the Bible:
Biblical Hermeneutics and Social Justice," *African Theology Today* 1 (2002b); *Other Ways of
Reading: African Women and the Bible*, Global Perspectives on Biblical Scholarship 2 (Atlanta:
Society of Biblical Literature), 2001; Philomenah Njeri Mwaura, "Feminist Biblical Interpreta-
tion and the Hermeneutics of Liberation: An African Woman's Perspective," in *Feminist Inter-
pretation of the Bible and the Hermeneutics of Liberation*, ed. S. Schroer and S. Bietenhard
(Sheffield: Sheffield Academic Press, 2003), 77-85; Sarojini Nadar, "On Being Pentecostal
Church: Pentecostal Women's Voices and Visions," in *On Being Church: African Women's Voices
and Visions*, ed. I. A. Phiri and S. Nadar (Geneva: WCC, 2005), 60-79; "Rereading Job in the
Midst of Suffering in the HIV/AIDS Era: How Not to Talk of God," *Old Testament Essays* 16
(2003): 343-57.

[16]Patriarchy is here defined, using the feminist historian Gerda Lerner's definition, as "the mani-
festation and institutionalization of male dominance over women and children in the family
and the extension of male dominance over women in the society in general." Gerda Lerner,
The Creation of Patriarchy (New York: Oxford University Press, 1986), 239.

regarding promoting justice and support for life and the dignity of women."[17] Mbuvi notes that the end of apartheid heralded a need for reconstruction. The 1990s and 2000s saw an increase of African biblical scholarship focusing on postexilic biblical literature, particularly that of Ezra and Nehemiah.[18] However, from the 2000s to the present day, postcolonial biblical interpretation has dominated the scene.[19] A postcolonial analysis focuses on the global problem of power asymmetries resulting from European colonialism. As practiced by African postcolonial interpreters, the approach is used to interpret the Bible so as to interrogate colonial assumptions present within the biblical texts and Euro-American interpretations of the biblical books.

MY OWN CONTEXTUAL APPROACH

As a diasporic Afro-feminist-womanist scholar (with a hyphenated identity), I locate my hermeneutical lens within the multifaceted space of Afro-womanist-feminist selfhood. My struggle is emancipatory and in the service of dignity, self-respect, and a radical transformation of situations of oppression and exclusion. The tri-polar Afro-feminist-womanist paradigm offers an essential avenue for exposing and

---

[17]Musimbi A. Kanyoro, *Introducing Feminist Cultural Hermeneutics: An African Perspective* (Sheffield: Sheffield Academic Press, 2002), 26.

[18]The term *postexilic* refers to the period of Jewish history after the Babylonian exile or captivity around 538 BCE. For an example of reading through the lens of postexilic hermeneutics, see Mbuvi, "African Biblical Studies," 163; Jesse Ndwiga Kanyua Mugambi, *From Liberation to Reconstruction* (Nairobi: East African Education Publishers, 1995); Elelwani Farisani, "The Use of Ezra–Nehemiah in a Quest for an African Theology of Reconstruction," *JTSA* 116 (2003): 27-50.

[19]Thus the analytical approach engages the "relationships of domination and subordination that were created in modern imperialism [and] did not end when geographical independence was won." Dube, *The HIV and AIDS Bible* (Scranton, PA: University of Scranton Press, 2006), 183. For further resources on postcolonial African analysis, see Mbuvi, "African Biblical Studies," 161; Dube, *Postcolonial Feminist Interpretation of the Bible*, 2000; J. K. Kinyua, "A Postcolonial Analysis of Bible Translation and Its Effectiveness in Shaping and Enhancing the Discourse of Colonialism and the Discourse of Resistance: The Gikuyu New Testament—a Case Study," *Black Theology* 11 (2013): 58-95; R. S. Wafula, *Biblical Representations of Moab: A Kenyan Postcolonial Reading*, Bible and Theology in Africa 19 (New York: Peter Lang, 2014); Kenneth Ngwa, "The Making of Gershom's Story: A Cameroonian Postwar Hermeneutics Reading of Exodus 2," *JBL* 134 (2015): 855-76.

investigating the multifaceted and intersecting realities of African women's intersecting inequalities. This tri-polar approach emphasizes the intertwining of different axes of Black women's oppression and assumes that Black women's oppression and social inequalities differ depending on their social locations. It aims at holding in dynamic tension my unique lived experiences and intersectional identities as an African Black woman with the converging experiences of women across cultures and social locations.[20] As highlighted earlier, while there are various methodological approaches in African biblical scholarship, the common denominator that unites the various interpretive programs is a commitment to relate biblical scholarship to flesh-and-blood African readers' lived realities. As such, the African context and its cultural and religious traditions are foundational to my analysis.

Essentially, therefore, this section argues for an approach to biblical interpretation that allows multiple plausible readings of texts to coexist. This means that there might be two or more justifiable readings of the loving neighbor story and the book of Esther, to take a case in point, each operating based on a somewhat different premise and interpretive logic. Of course, some readings of the stories might be more plausible than others—some that I will subscribe to and some that I will dispute—but I do not consider my interpretation of the text to be final and uniquely authoritative. As Brian Blount rightly notes, "Each interpretation is a single piece of a larger picture of potential meaning, and therefore represents an acquisition of only a segment of that potential."[21] Therefore, my proposed reading of these two texts, using an African contextual lens, is not proposed as the whole picture. I fundamentally believe that, even though multiple and perhaps competing interpretations of the same text can coexist, it is appropriate and useful to convey a specific preferred understanding of a text. A contextually preferred argument is not the same thing as

---

[20] Alice Yafeh-Deigh, *Paul's Sexual and Marital Ethics in 1 Corinthians 7: An African-Cameroonian Perspective*, Bible and Theology in Africa 22 (New York: Peter Lang, 2015).
[21] Blount, *Cultural Interpretation*, 90.

establishing and promoting a single authoritative analysis. In light of this, African biblical scholars, including myself, use cultural and postcolonial critical strategies to interrogate, expose, and disrupt the singularity and centrality of those Eurocentric historical-critical interpretations that seek to establish their analysis and worldview as solely authoritative. With the aforesaid, let us now turn our attention to the biblical text.

STOP AND THINK

- What are some of the specific gender-role expectations of your social location? How do the expectations inform those preconceived notions you bring to the Bible?

- In what ways do you read the Bible through the lens of your culture? What tensions between text and interpretive context do you encounter?

- How might we understand the parable of the loving neighbor differently if we foreground it within the empire and patriarchal relationships?

READING TEXTS

One of our primary purposes for writing this book is to provide students opportunities to hear interpreters' voices from culturally and religiously diverse social locations reading texts from the Bible. In today's pluralistic world, and particularly in the current age of globalization, Bible readers need to be fully informed about multidimensional approaches for engaging with Christian Scripture. This multifaceted approach to reading the Bible must include a range of non-Western perspectives. Pedagogically, instructors of the Bible are challenged to move beyond interpretations prescribed by mainstream Eurocentric scholarship to include views from various contexts. In this section, the parable of the loving neighbor and the book of Esther will be analyzed through Afro-Cameroonian sociocultural and religious realities.

The Parable of the Loving Neighbor (Luke 10:25-37)

On the surface, the parable's moral import about the loving neighbor appears self-evident (a call to emulate his virtue of hospitality); however, close readings of the passage have underscored it as a densely woven tapestry with multiple interpretive possibilities. In this section, I will bring an African contextual hermeneutical strategy to bear on my analysis of the loving neighbor story. To be more specific, I will read the story from the social location of the Ngoketunjia Division, a region located in the Northwest Region of Cameroon, with a particular focus on the Ndop plain subdivision of the Ngoketunjia

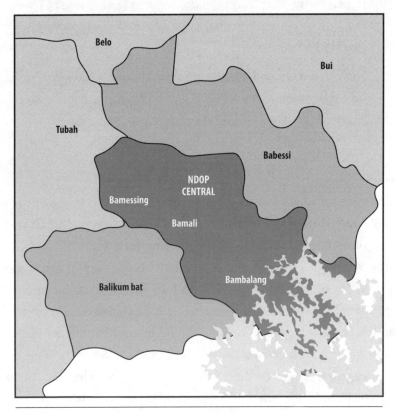

The Ndop subdivision in Cameroon

Division. The questions I will be asking of the text are questions generated from the lived experiences of the Ndop people.[22] The goal here is to offer a contemporary-contextual assessment of the story, reconceptualized sociopolitically as a story that addresses the concrete realities of intra-ethnic and inter-ethnic conflicts in this unique locale.

Interpretive context: Ndop subdivision, Ngoketunjia Division, Northwest Region of Cameroon. As one of the divisions that make up the Northwest Region of Cameroon, the Ngoketunjia Division has its central city in Bamuka in the Ndop subdivision. Thirteen villages make up the division. A traditional ruler called a *Fon* rules each of the communities. Although English is the common language in the Ngoketunjia Division, each of the thirteen villages has its distinct language and cultural traditions. These linguistic and cultural differences have led to multilevel discrimination and prejudices. It is widely known in Cameroon that the Ngoketunjia Division is riddled with inter- and intra-ethnic squabbles. Bias, stereotyping, and misperception are unavoidable features of daily living among tribal groups in this division. Whereas ethno-religious tensions and disputes were the bedrock of the Jew/Samaritan conflict, quarrels over land, which usually lead to intertribal wars, are the core of inter-ethnic conflicts in the Ngoketunjia Division, as in Cameroon in general. It is the root of tribal conflicts in the division, particularly because the populations survive mainly on subsistence agriculture. Often, land conflicts result from fluid boundaries that are either colonial leftovers or boundaries created during wartime. Besides land disputes, ethnic prejudices and negative stereotypes are widespread in these tribal communities. Distinctive group identity and characteristics sustain and reinforce the stereotypes, leading to social exclusion. Given that Christian communities in the Ngoketunjia place the sacred authority of Scripture as head of their beliefs and moral behavior, their scathing indictment of stereotypes and prejudices and their instruction to emulate the noble

---

[22]I recognize here that the constituent communities in Ndop are pluralistic.

example of the Samaritan are particularly crucial within contexts like those of Ndop.

Reading the loving neighbor story within the Ngoketunjia social location. In its narrative context, the parable of the loving neighbor is located within Luke's travel narrative (Luke 9:51–19:27). Jesus himself is traveling the dangerous road to his death in Jerusalem. Meanwhile, he selflessly focuses on discipleship formation through a variety of teaching strategies. Within the context of Jesus' journey, the loving neighbor's parable is an educational story meant to elicit change in perception and lifestyle.

The story begins with a certain lawyer asking Jesus how he could inherit eternal life (Luke 10:25-28). It ends with Jesus' challenge to the addressee and audience to go act as neighbors (Luke 10:37).[23] The parable itself (Luke 10:29b-37) is set in a dangerous location, the road from Jerusalem to Jericho.[24] The parable is itself triggered by, and in answer to, a question posed by the lawyer ("Who is my neighbor?"). Jesus responds with a story that disrupts and problematizes commonly held assumptions about a neighbor. He seeks to reorient and transform how the lawyer and readers think and behave vis-à-vis an ethnic and religious "Other."

Jesus has just mostly summed up the law within the framework of the commandments to love God and love one's neighbor (Luke 10:25-28; Matthew 22:34-40; and Mark 12:28-34), the keeping of which is assumed to be crucial and indispensable for gaining eternal life. Unsatisfied by Jesus' answer and desiring to create boundaries around "neighbor" (*plēsion*, a noun contextually carrying multiple meanings), the lawyer's "Who is my neighbor?"

---

[23]We have to distinguish between the addressee of Jesus' parable and the audience. By addressees, I mean the specific target person/group that the implied author had in mind. The audience of the discourse is all who hear and read the parable. Jesus is telling the parable distinctively as a response to the lawyer's query regarding the neighbor. Though not targeted, however, it can be inferred that Jesus expects an active response from the disciples and all readers.

[24]While the history of the Jew/Samaritan conflict is pertinent to this discussion, space does not allow me to engage it entirely. See the excursus in chapter 2 of this volume.

signals that he wants Jesus to explain its meaning for him. The broad semantic range or possible sense of the noun notwithstanding, the lawyer cannot imagine a Samaritan fitting within the scope of the noun's plausible meanings. Samaritans were not viewed as part of the covenant people of God; therefore, they could not conceivably qualify as "neighbor." Jesus does not define for the lawyer who a neighbor is; instead, through the actions of the Samaritan, he gives criteria for identifying and becoming a neighbor (Luke 10:37a). Fundamentally, Jesus reframes and transforms the lawyer's query into how to act in such a way that one is identified as a neighbor.[25] Such a reframing of the lawyer's question does not dismiss the original question altogether but rightly locates it in its appropriate praxis-focused context, the broader context.[26] By so doing, Jesus radicalizes his definition of neighbor, effectively unmasking and confronting prejudicial and stereotypic attitudes and behaviors that delimit insider/outsider boundaries. The Samaritan's brave actions show that the cost of discipleship is high.

In the parable, an ethnic and religious other, who is viewed as the enemy, engages in an emergency response propelled by irresistible compassion (*esplanchnisthē*, Luke 10:33), unconcerned about his safety. As underscored by the details of his generous actions ("bandaged his wounds, pouring on oil and wine . . . he put the man on his donkey, took him to an inn and took care of him," Luke 10:33-35), the Samaritan treated the stripped, bleeding, and half-dead man with respect, honor, and dignity. The Samaritan confers honor on the assaulted man in the way he nurses him. Besides, by highlighting the fact that the Samaritan acted with extreme care toward the victim, Jesus acknowledges the

---

[25]This is exemplified by Jesus' praxis-oriented response to John's question in Luke 7:18-23. Jesus did not give a theoretical answer to the question addressed to him by John through his disciples. Instead, he pointed to the transformative and restorative activities taking place as signs that underscore the activities of the kingdom and nature of messiahship.

[26]A praxis-oriented or praxis-focused story correlates theory and practice. The reader naturally makes a practical judgment on how to act in the situation presented in the story. As such, practical application is always on the horizon of all stories or theories.

Samaritan's exceptionally selfless generosity. The Samaritan's actions as a neighbor are a model of what is expected of a neighbor. Intense love and compassion allow for the permeability of group boundaries.

By not identifying the robbed and assaulted victim with a particular ethnic or social group but intentionally leaving him in complete anonymity ("a man"), the text universalizes the term *neighbor* to imply any person. This unspecified ethnicity opens up a new sphere of imaginative and hermeneutical possibilities. For example, it allows a reader from the Ndop social location to discover parallels between the Jew/Samaritan conflicts of the biblical world and the current tribal conflicts among Ndop social groups in the contemporary world. The Samaritan is revealed to the Ndop social group as a role model, the quintessential example of neighborly behavior, and an antithesis to prejudice, stereotypes, and discrimination.

As the story ends, "the original question, 'Who is my neighbor?' (10:29), shifts to 'Which of these three acted as neighbor to the person who fell into the hands of the robbers?' (10:36)."[27] Jesus invites the lawyer to assess the character of the priest, Levite, Samaritan, and their actions (Luke 10:36). Given that a Samaritan social group member performs activities that disconfirm the lawyer's stereotypical and negative assessment of the Samaritans, his evaluation of this Samaritan changes. As such, he can recognize that the Samaritan acted like a neighbor. The story unambiguously chastises the Levite, priest, lawyer, and audience for their indifference to human suffering. The injunction to "go and do likewise" (Luke 10:37) places a moral obligation on the audience to emulate the Samaritan's altruistic compassion. Primarily, Jesus uses shock rhetoric to prompt the audience to feel empathy for the Samaritan, the stigmatized "other." Shock rhetoric is necessary for situations where attitudes toward a particular group are notoriously hard to change. It is not a call to treat this

---

[27]Anne Elvey, "Rethinking Neighbour Love: A Conversation Between Political Theology and Ecological Ethics," in *Where the Wild Ox Roams: Biblical Essays in Honour of Norman C. Habel*, ed. Alan Cadwallader and Peter Trudinger (Sheffield: Sheffield Phoenix, 2013), 72.

specific Samaritan as an exception that does not change the rule, but a call for a complete change of how the lawyer and all readers view the world and how to relate to the other.

By portraying the Samaritan as the hospitable other, Jesus sets him up as a model for transgressing stereotypical boundaries. His admonition to the Jewish lawyer to "go and do likewise" (Luke 10:37b) is not only an ethical challenge and an invitation to the lawyer and his socio-ethnic group, but it is also a moral challenge across all ethnic groups. It is equally a challenge for readers to practice introspection in order to search out their potential prejudicial tendencies. Jesus wants humaneness to constitute an essential element in influencing believers' everyday lives. He presents a praxis-oriented lifestyle as a Christ-centered model of discipleship rooted in the double commandment of love for God and love for neighbor (cf. Deuteronomy 6:5; Leviticus 19:18; Matthew 22:36-39; Mark 12:28-31).

Jesus ends the story with a prophetic challenge and call to action for restorative justice. Jesus' kingdom praxis in the Gospel of Luke is centered decisively on social repair, rehabilitation, and inclusion for those who are permanently confined to lives of social exclusion and marginalization. The parable of the loving neighbor reframes the essentials of Jesus' ministry in terms of social justice, fundamentally reoriented as restorative justice on behalf of all marginalized, oppressed, and excluded persons. Jesus' transgressive boundary-crossing behaviors offer an alternative way of envisioning interpersonal relationships between people from different cultural groups. People who belong to God's covenant community are called to transcend the boundaries of gender, culture, ethnicity, race, religion, and class, to name a few.

As a scathing indictment of stereotypes and prejudices, the subversive content turns the lawyer's world and the audience upside down, giving them an outlet for self-criticism. Since religion plays a central role in Cameroonian-Ndop social and cultural groups' identity constructions, contemporary Ndop readers must hear the story speaking to them as it did to Luke's audience. "Go and do likewise" is a clarion call that moves the story beyond its social, cultural, and historical specificity. To those living in the Ndop/Ngoketunjia Division, it forces us to think critically about the interpersonal relationships between neighboring tribes. Acting like the Samaritan in this context could mean helping change the relationship between neighboring tribes through a categorical restructuring of intertribal relations.

Vashti and Esther: Complementary Models of Resistance

In addition to how other biblical scholars have interacted with the book of Esther, I propose an example of a contextual reading informed by the lived experiences, cultural practices, and worldviews of African women, particularly Cameroonian women. I will not delve into all the details of the book of Esther. I limit my analysis to Vashti's and Esther's characterizations, and the implications of such descriptions for contemporary readers in Cameroon, specifically women in Bamessing, Ndop. This narrow focus will undoubtedly overlook other details of the story. I will use Cameroonian women's cultural understandings of gender and gender-role expectations as the lens through which I propose a contextual reading of Vashti's and Esther's characters. My evaluation of Vashti's and Esther's representations will investigate how the intersecting experiences of ethnicity, nationality, religion, class, gender, cultural beliefs, and diasporic belonging combine to form their identity.[28]

Reading as a postcolonial feminist from my Cameroonian social location, Esther's book is best construed through an intersectional lens that foregrounds Esther's multiple identity markers.[29] An

---

[28]Nadar Sarojini, "'Texts of Terror': The Conspiracy of Rape in the Bible, Church, and Society: The Case of Esther 2:1-18," in *African Women, Religion and Health: Essays in Honor of Mercy Amba Ewudziwa Oduyoye*, ed. Isabel A. Phiri and Sarojini Nadar (Pietermaritzburg: Cluster Publications, 2006), 77-95.

[29]*Intersectionality* is an umbrella term that provides an analytical framework and vocabulary for conceptualizing various axes of oppression. It highlights the complex multidimensionality of identity. Kimberlé Crenshaw coined the term as an analytical tool to address Black women's intersecting inequalities. See Kimberlé Crenshaw, "Demarginalizing the Intersection of

intersectional analysis acknowledges the complex multidimensional strands of Vashti's and Esther's characterizations. As such, both women cannot be easily categorized as either a disruption of or conformity to the status quo. Esther, the protagonist, is a woman, a Jew, an orphan, a queen, an exile, and a stranger who must survive displacement in a diasporic patriarchal world. Multiple stigmatized identities—ethnicity, gender, class—converge in her, and they are interconnected in complex ways. Esther's character analysis, even if focusing on gender justice discussions, must include a critical awareness or reflection on her overlapping identity markers to account adequately for complexity in the way the narrative characterizes her. The complexities in the way Esther is portrayed in the story are compounded by the fact that she is placed at the intersection of oppression and privilege.

Like Esther, many African women experience multiple forms of overlapping oppressions, social identities, and social relations. Their experience of gender injustice intersects with other distinct disadvantages and lived experiences. Their discrimination experiences are based on gender, ethnicity, social status, age, marital status, and many more identity markers. Undeniably, African women's lived experiences differ depending on their distinctive social locations and historical moments. However, there is solidarity and some common characteristics while acknowledging the differences among them. Stated differently, some experiences link African women together

---

Race and Sex: A Black Feminist Critique of Antidiscrimination Doctrine, Feminist Theory, and Antiracist Politics," *University of Chicago Legal Forum* 1 (1989): 139-67. As Paulette Caldwell avers, "Racism and sexism are interlocking, mutually reinforcing components of a system of dominance rooted in patriarchy. No significant and lasting progress in combating either can be made until this interdependence is acknowledged, and until the perspectives gained from considering their interaction are reflected in legal theory and public policy" ("A Hair Piece: Perspectives on the Intersection of Race and Gender," in *Critical Race Theory: The Cutting Edge*, ed. R. Delgado [Philadelphia: Temple University Press, 1995], 267). Intersectionality provides a practical framework for investigating Esther's multilayered experiences within the Persian Empire. In this paper, a robust analysis of Esther's identity intersections is impossible due to my focus on gender analysis, but the intersections need to be acknowledged.

across cultures and social locations. For instance, their experiences converge on the core issue of African women's crosscultural subordination within institutional structures of patriarchy and androcentrism. Another common core is the colonial experience and the realities of living in postcolonial societies where gender discrimination is institutionalized and normalized.

My goal in this section is to contextualize Esther's narrative within the ongoing gender justice discussions among African women and critically examine the contextual variables informing African women's reading of Vashti's and Esther's story. The purpose is to show that the culture, particularly its gender-role expectations, is not dramatically different from those of contemporary African women. Patriarchy and gender-role stereotypes are issues of the ancient Near East's cultural milieu and also a present reality for African women. African women across the continent are still socially disadvantaged, and gender-based inequities intersect with other patriarchal societal axes of power. As in the Persian Empire, patriarchal gender norms also provide the historical underpinnings of discriminatory attitudes against African women. As such, the story of Vashti and Esther resonates well with those of African women.

The premise here is that, when assessed in terms of gender norms, Vashti's and Esther's characters are evaluated differently in different sociopolitical and cultural contexts. Within the African context, some women view Esther as the antithesis of Vashti's assertiveness. In their view, Esther is the quintessential wife and queen, who readily conforms to gender expectations or stereotypes. To other women, Vashti is an example of a strong African woman who is not afraid to be obstinate and defiant, regardless of the consequences. Vashti's resistance to the king's attempt to sexually objectify her by publicly displaying her beauty (Esther 1:10-12) makes Vashti a positive model for independent African women, even when her assertive approach is not effective at promoting social change. I show here that both women should be held up to represent different resistance models for African women. I assert that Esther is a victim of multilayered patriarchal stereotypes and prejudices concerning gender norms and expectations. She has many intersectional areas of discrimination that are part of her lived experiences. Esther's story works subversively as a story of a woman who, despite her seeming compliance with the status quo, worked the patriarchal system to ensure that she saved her Jewish people from Haman's xenophobic genocidal plot. Thus, it is not merely a story about gender and sexual politics; it is, like Vashti's, a survival story.

Interpretive synopsis of the book of Esther. The geographical, cultural, and sociopolitical setting of the book of Esther is Susa, the winter capital of the Persian Empire. The book opens in an ancient Near Eastern patriarchal Persian court with an enormous royal banquet thrown by King Ahasuerus (or Xerxes I, Esther 1:1-4) for the noblemen from his provinces that lasts six months (180 days). Queen Vashti gave a banquet for women in the royal house during Ahasuerus's second banquet (Esther 1:5-9). On the second banquet's final day, Ahasuerus, inebriated, orders Vashti to wear her crown and display/parade her beauty in front of the king's male banquet guests. Vashti refuses to appear and assuage the king's ego (Esther 1:10-12), a decision that defies patriarchal gender-role expectations. She takes a subversive stance against the objectification of her body.[30]

Deeply humiliated and infuriated by Vashti's defiant behavior (Esther 1:12), King Ahasuerus consults the royal sages. They suggest he make a public example of the rebellious Queen Vashti

---

[30]Masenya Madipoane argues that Vashti is stripped of agency in the story: "Vashti never really appears as an independent character at all, except when she breaks the code of conduct by refusing to appear before the king, an act that culminates in her removal from the scene. Like an exile in a foreign country, Vashti cannot be allowed to possess her own will. She can only survive through being assimilated by patriarchy. Vashti is a stranger in what is supposed to be her territory." Masenya Madipoane, "Their Hermeneutics Was Strange! Ours Is a Necessity! Reading Vashti in Esther 1 as African Women in South Africa," in *Her Master's Tools? Feminist and Postcolonial Engagements of Historical-Critical Discourse*, ed. Caroline Vander Stichele and Todd Penner, Global Perspectives on Biblical Scholarship 9 (Atlanta: SBL, 2005), 191.

(Esther 1:13-22). Vashti's public humiliation served as a cautionary emergency strategy to teach all women the brutal consequences of nonconformity to prescribed gender roles. Ahasuerus, publicly shamed by Vashti's defiance, issues a proclamation divorcing Vashti and banning her from his presence. The explicit purpose of Vashti's indictment is to dissuade women from emulating her. The feminist slogan, "the personal is political," resonates nicely with the narrative, as Vashti's refusal to appear before Ahasuerus is now politicized and transformed into a national crisis (Esther 1:17-18). The decree is written as a moralistic lesson to ensure that "all women will honor their husbands, high and low alike" (Esther 1:20). The message is couched to endorse, solidify, instill, and legitimize patriarchally structured relationships ("every man should be master in his own house," Esther 1:22). The missive implies the empire's need for a subordinate and subservient queen. Persia needs a queen who can be kept under patriarchal supervision. The decree helps reinforce the message of female inferiority and subjugation.

Vashti is dethroned, villainized, and banished permanently from the king's presence.[31] She abruptly disappears from the plot of the story. Vashti is replaced by a beautiful young virgin, Esther, an orphan, adopted by her Jewish cousin Mordecai (Esther 2:5-6). Esther's acquiescence and compliance to the normative patriarchal beauty/sex contest arrangements aimed at selecting a new virgin wife for the king leads to her ascendance to the throne as a replacement for Vashti (Esther 2:8-18). Unlike Vashti, who is more threatening to the status quo, Esther is a devoted and seemingly submissive woman who does not pose a threat to the patriarchal order.

---

[31]The removal of Vashti from the throne and erasure from the narrative plot is so early and sudden that the reader does not have much information about her intersectional identity. Although patriarchal social structures are male-centered and are shaped by the different matrix of power and domination, patriarchal institutions are not homogeneous in their gender-role expectations. Also, women's experiences of oppression within patriarchal social structures cannot be essentialized. All social structures of patriarchy create and reproduce gender-based inequalities.

As the story progresses, Esther transforms into a confident, independent woman with strong leadership potential. When Haman's xenophobic hostility and spite vis-à-vis Mordecai translates into a political and national antagonism toward the Jewish people (Esther 3:5-6), Esther begins to assume an autonomous leadership role (Esther 4:16-17). When the conflict escalates into a national crisis (Esther 3:6-11), due primarily to Haman's campaign of genocide (Esther 3:13), Mordecai effectively captures Esther's heart through a rhetorical appeal to her emotions using manipulative threats (Esther 4:13-17). A significant threat is the claim that "if you keep silence at such a time as this, relief and deliverance will arise for the Jews from another quarter, but you and your father's family will perish. Who knows? Perhaps you have come to royal dignity for just such a time as this" (Esther 4:14). Persuaded by Mordecai's indictment speech, Esther confronts her fears and ventures into a dangerous situation of possible death by appearing before the king unsummoned (Esther 5:1-2).

Esther takes matters into her own hands after grappling with the competing claims' weight on her loyalty. She assumes control of the situation, sets the plan, and does most of the talking, instructing Mordecai (Esther 4:16). She will plead with the king but on her terms, after fasting from food and drink for three days. Esther appears before the king unsummoned and intercedes with the king on behalf of her people. She ultimately discloses and reverses Haman's plans and saves the Jewish people from Haman's tactically planned genocide (Esther 6:1-14). Her passionate appeal to the king's emotions (Esther 7:3-4) made it possible for her to effect liberation for the Jewish people (Esther 9:1-9), create political change (Esther 9:20–10:3), and ultimately become a national heroine. As Bonna Devora Haberman aptly contends, Esther's action to save her people "indicates her gradual ascent to power and the possibility of feminist activism."[32] She proves her prowess as a leader in a male-dominated

---

[32]Bonna Devora Haberman, "Unmasking the Scroll of Esther," *Tikkun* 17 (2002): 49.

social structure by becoming a harbinger of change and an instrument for national deliverance.

An Afro-Cameroonian evaluation of the story. The narrator of
the book of Esther tells the story so that Vashti and Esther are pitted
against each other in a male-dominated patriarchal structure. In the
first three chapters of the narrative, the narrator's worldview appears
to be legitimated. Vashti is set up as a foil for Esther, the titular protagonist. At first, Esther is characterized as a nondefiant woman who
consents to oppressive stereotypes and attitudes.[33] Esther's submissive character and virtues serve as contrasting qualities to the
flaws of Vashti. Vashti's character also serves to progress the book; it
is her place as a foil that is most significant. Immediately after Esther's
entrance into the narrative as the new protagonist (Esther 2:17-18),
for example, Vashti disappears from the plot of the story, but her
shadow does not. The shadow cast by her unjust circumstances is
interwoven with the competing story about Esther. Vashti's refusal
to be sexually objectified and humiliated by her drunken husband is
perceived perennially by some feminist critics as the paradigmatic
example of female rebelliousness, stubbornness, resentment, and
conscious disobedience. Her insubordinate action is shocking and
embarrassing to her male contemporaries because it is not normative,
and she is quickly deposed. Even with Vashti's departure, however,
the female body's objectification continues in Esther's description.
Because both women live in a patriarchal culture that sexually objec-
tifies the female body, Esther is equally vulnerable to sexual objectification. Her worth is equated with her body's appearance: "The girl
was fair and beautiful" (Esther 2:7). Her value is based on her

---

[33]The verbs used to describe her underscore her character as a passive, submissive, dutiful, and
obedient woman. She is taken into the king's palace and is put in the custody of Hegai
(Esther 2:8); Mordecai charged her not to reveal her Jewish identity (Esther 2:10); she was
taken to King Ahasuerus, who raped her (Esther 2:16); the king set the royal crown on her
head and made her a replacement for Vashti (Esther 2:17); Mordecai charged Esther to go to
the king and solicit help on behalf of the Jews (Esther 4:8); Mordecai threatened Esther if she
stayed silent (Esther 4:13-14). Such characterization makes her a perfect foil for Vashti.

physicality, which perpetuates and reinforces the patriarchal ide-
ology of female objectification. She wins the king's heart based on
her appearance. Traditional gender-role socialization encourages
Esther to relinquish her agency and dignity through passive sub-
mission to her powerful, controlling, and dominant husband who
uses her as a sexual object. Accordingly, she must spend the night
with the king before being deemed worthy of being his wife—the
king and his entourage view sex as a conquest. At the end of the story,
even though she risks her life to protect her ethnic group, the narrative deprives her of the highest honor and instead credits Mordecai
as the hero of the story (Esther 10:3). Esther and Vashti's difference
is that "Vashti is one woman confronted in male space with many
men as judges; Esther is among many women confronted in female
space with one man as a judge."[34]

By focusing on the "drama" created by Vashti's behavior and her
subsequent replacement by an initially passive and submissive Esther,
readers often overlook the fact that class, ethnicity, and gender are
interlocking systems of discrimination in the story. Esther's character
is usually assessed in the context of gender stereotypes and prejudice
only. However, to capture her identity's multifaceted and complex
nature, Esther's character must be viewed through a more robust intersecting lens that encompasses gender, sexuality, politics, culture,
and religion. Vashti and Esther are both powerful role models who,
in very distinct ways, inspire thousands of African women in their
fight against patriarchal discrimination. They are two victims trapped
in the boundaries set by male-defined and male-controlled systems,
yet they assert themselves publicly. Their behavior defies the male
boundaries and subverts their oppressive social and institutional
structures. Despite cultural variations, all African patriarchal societies regulate and dictate women's fate because of the intrinsic belief

---

[34]Lillian R. Klein, *From Deborah to Esther: Sexual Politics in the Hebrew Bible* (Minneapolis:
Fortress, 2003), 102.

that women are men's property. It is an ignored fact that in a male-dominated, male-centered culture, women encounter a spectrum of violence daily. Both Vashti and Esther may be looked to as different models of resistance. Each disrupts patriarchal structures in different ways. Although they are often seen as antitheses, they exhibit rather complementary modes of responses to patriarchal ideologies, structures, and practices.

As Itumeleng Mosala rightly notes, the narrative's primary issue is "the gendered structuring of politics."[35] The oppression of women in Cameroon correlates with the gendered structuring of politics in Esther. Women in Cameroon are struggling daily against culturally based practices and beliefs that are harmful to women. Sexual victimization is commonplace, particularly among women of Bamessing, Ndop, the social location from which I am reading. Many women experience extreme forms of sexual assault and sexual harassment that are legitimated by the patriarchal system. Just as patriarchy limited women's roles in ancient Near Eastern Persia, the culture in which the book of Esther was written, patriarchy restricts women's roles in a multitude of ways in Bamessing. In Ndop patriarchal cultures, traditional gender-role socialization forces many women to internalize sexist oppression. They are expected to comply with the decisions and demands made by men. Battery, sexual harassment, and a spectrum of domestic violence abuses are commonplace and ignored due to power asymmetries, particularly related to gender power relations. Women who are beaten up by their husbands are often made to take responsibility for their husbands' actions (a blame-the-victim mentality). Women whose behavior defies gender stereotypes live in social marginalization and exclusion.

Vashti's character helps unmask and challenge gender-based violence for vulnerable and powerless women who lack agency and

[35]Itumeleng Mosala, "The Implications of the Text of Esther for African Women's Struggle for Liberation in South Africa," in *The Postcolonial Biblical Reader*, ed. R. S. Sugirtharajah (Oxford: Blackwell, 2008), 138.

public voice. She is a model of one who suffers gender-based violence because of oppressive patriarchal structures. By not conforming to gendered expectations, Vashti becomes a symbol of courage and a positive role model for all Bamessing women who are victims of patriarchy and male violence. Vashti's characterization provides a paradigm for understanding the vulnerabilities experienced by many independent African/Bamessing women. African men raised in patriarchal family structures, in which traditional gender roles are encouraged, see independent women as community threats. The danger they pose influences other women to defy their roles as passive and submissive, controlled by their husbands. Accordingly, cultural expectations around gender roles are mostly the same in ancient Near Eastern cultures as in most African/Bamessing communities.

In the patriarchal system of Bamessing, there is a group of women for whom Vashti's refusal to appear before the king is a sign of disrespect. Her attitude is shocking and too unconventional. For them, Vashti is wrong to deny the king's sexually objectifying demand. This group of women is unfazed by the sexual objectification implied in the king's decision to parade Vashti before his party guests. The rationale is that a respectful attitude toward men is expected of all women, even if they face being sexually controlled and assaulted. The patriarchal family structure creates an environment that normalizes discrimination and violence against women. Many African/Cameroonian women have internalized social norms that hold that their marital status should be subordinate. Since these women have co-opted androcentric and patriarchal ideologies as normative and natural, they read the book of Esther through the stereotyped conceptions of gender roles in Cameroon. Maligning Vashti's insubordination, they do not see her in a sympathetic light. Instead, they chastise her for refusing to submit herself to patriarchal expectations of women. Vashti is reprimanded for not being a passive, obedient, and submissive wife; they state no one empathizes with her because she is not a good role model, nor is she worthy of emulation. On the contrary, Esther is portrayed sympathetically throughout the narrative and is made to exemplify a good woman's traits.[36] Mainly, as Alice Laffey notes, the narrative presents her as "a stereotypical woman in a man's world"[37]; she represents the ideal African wife.

On the other hand, women with the potential of destabilizing such patriarchal ideals can truly understand Vashti's motivations and share their feelings. To them, Vashti is unquestionably a sympathetic character. She "can thus serve as a model for women who have been socialized to agree with everything said by their husbands/men."[38] Though stripped of her royal position, banished from the king's presence, and disenfranchised, Vashti maintains her dignity and autonomy. She "succeeded in showing the people and particularly the men of her time that women also have a will and can exercise that will whenever they want to, irrespective of what the consequences may be."[39] While she is moved away to society's fringes, where she experiences social exclusion and becomes vulnerable to adverse social and economic circumstances, she is remembered by many contemporary women as a model emancipated woman. As Clinton Moyer aptly notes, Vashti "is presented as an unstable force, a disruptor of the natural order of things."[40] Vashti's refusal to allow her body to be a site that attracts the male gaze, as an object of men's sexual pleasure, lays bare the insecurity and instability of male power. It reveals the impulse of patriarchy to maintain the status quo through female subordination.

---

[36]Madipoane Masenya, "'A Small Herb Increases Itself (Makes Impact) by a Strong Odour': Re-imagining Vashti in an African South African Context," in *Biblical Interpretation in African Perspective*, ed. David Tuesday Adamo (Lanham, MD: University Press of America, 2006), 88.

[37]Alice Laffey, *An Introduction to the Old Testament: A Feminist Perspective* (Philadelphia: Fortress Press, 1988), 216.

[38]Masenya, "A Small Herb Increases Itself," 95.

[39]Masenya, "A Small Herb Increases Itself," 96.

[40]Clinton Moyer, "The Beautiful Outsider Replaces the Queen: A 'Compound Topos' in Esther 1–2 and Books 5 and 6 of Chariton's *Chaereas and Callirhoe*," *Vetus Testamentum* 60 (2010): 608.

However, Vashti's refusal threatens male power. She took power away from men by reclaiming control over her body. Consequently, Vashti is the object of a terrible patriarchal punishment due to her decisive actions;[41] she is hastily deposed or demoted as queen and experiences exclusion and rejection with perhaps no restorative justice possibilities.

Like Vashti, most women in Bamessing, Ndop, are targets of sexual victimization, and thus their rights and dignity are not accorded equal respect and protection as are those of men. They live in a system where there are multiple barriers to society's full participation through discriminatory attitudes and behaviors. The normalization of male dominance over women is that many women experience coercive control over their bodies. Strong, independent women who resist and subvert patriarchal gender roles experience similar punishment to that of Vashti. Some are thrown out of their matrimonial homes without their children, abandoned by their families (because they do not want to return their bride price), and must fend for themselves. They survive because of their drive to transgress gender boundaries and challenge traditional patriarchal authority patterns. They develop for themselves coping strategies that help them navigate the system without male protectors.

As I mentioned earlier, viewed through an intersectional paradigm, both Vashti and Esther are role models to emulate in women's struggle for emancipation. Esther's character is also dynamic and multifaceted. The intersection of ethnicity and gender accounts for her complex personality. Although Esther is initially positioned in the narrative as conforming to gender stereotypes, she resists and subverts the power structures in subtle ways to transform her condition. When Esther is first introduced in the story in Esther 2 as a potential replacement for Vashti, she is predominantly characterized as obediently following Mordecai's strategic instructions and exhibiting attitudes befitting for

---

[41]Cf. Mmapula Diana Kebaneilwe, "The Vashti Paradigm Resistance as a Strategy for Combating HIV," *Ecumenical Review* 63 (2011): 378.

a good Persian queen (Esther 2:10). However, as the plot progresses, readers notice that she *is not always* conventional, compliant, selfless, and docile as she is often pigeonholed. Shortly after Queen Vashti is dethroned and banished, she too violates existing patriarchal conventions, risking her own life by intruding into a dangerous space, the king's presence, without being summoned. She summarizes her bold and courageous decision thus: "I will go to the king, even though it is against the law; and if I perish, I perish" (Esther 4:16). Esther makes her own precariously self-sacrificing choices and helps foil Haman's plan to annihilate the Jews. Once Haman overtly asserts himself as the "enemy of the Jews" and plots their genocide, Esther, fully aware of all the risks involved, discloses her Jewish identity (Esther 7:3-6), and then liberates her people from Haman's genocidal plot. Esther's bold, assertive, and decisive actions should be held in dynamic tension with her role as a meek, respectful, loyal, and dependent wife. Esther knows how to perform her culturally expected role of a submissive and obedient wife as well as using the power available to her as the queen to undermine patriarchal conventions and sway the king's emotions to her advantage (Esther 5:2-8). Consequently, Esther inspires African women and is a role model in their struggle for social change and gender justice.

Many African women stay in oppressive marital homes because they rely on the patriarchal household to survive. With discriminatory laws, policies, and oppressive traditional customs firmly in place that ensures women have no access to property ownership or land inheritance, most African women have no hope of survival outside oppressive patriarchal structures. The intersectional experiences of discrimination based on gender and class limit African women's abilities to resist the patriarchal status quo. Instead of reinforcing stereotypes of women, as is often thought, Esther is a positive role model for women struggling to survive within entrenched patriarchal family structures. Although many feel trapped in oppressive marriages, they do not overtly rebel against the system, a strategy Angeline Song calls the "pragmatism of the powerless."[42] Instead, like Esther, they embrace their traditional role as wives by acquiescing to normative, socially sanctioned female behaviors and practices while equally using their reimagined position as wives to challenge the status quo and disrupt patriarchal boundaries.[43] Essentially, being "shrewd, pragmatic, and patient may be more useful . . . than a fruitless act of overt disobedience."[44] Esther's model thus speaks to groups of women in Ndop who must survive within the constraints of contemporary patriarchal structures of discrimination and oppression.

From the above, one can posit that African women hold up Esther as an exemplary woman, not because she conforms to patriarchal gender roles but because she is an example of how a woman can survive in a male-dominated world without escaping the confines of patriarchy. Vashti epitomizes a strong, assertive, independent woman who openly confronts patriarchy and pushes against the confines of prescribed gender roles. However, Esther is not the antithesis of Vashti. Together, both women represent different models of resistance within the male power structures of the story.

REFLECTING ON THE TEXTS

- What contextual variables inform your reading of the loving neighbor story?

- How might the loving neighbor story motivate you to be a neighbor to someone radically different from you in terms of ethnicity, race, class, culture, and religion?

- Do you see anything intriguing in the way that Vashti and Esther are portrayed in the book of Esther? What are

---

[42]Angeline Song, "Heartless Bimbo or Subversive Role Model? A Narrative (Self) Critical Reading of the Character of Esther," *Dialog* 49 (2010): 60.
[43]Cf. Song, "Heartless Bimbo or Subversive Role Model?," 59.
[44]Song, "Heartless Bimbo or Subversive Role Model?," 59.

some of the specific gender-role expectations of your
social location?

- How do the expectations inform the preunderstanding
  you bring to the story of Esther? What tensions does the
  story embody? How might we understand this story
  differently if we foreground it within the empire and
  patriarchal relationships?

CONCLUDING THOUGHTS

I began this chapter with a premise, by now very familiar, that interpreters from a variety of contexts read the Bible differently because of
the particularities of their social locations and the specific interpretive
strategy used. It is taken for granted that all texts are contextually
produced. All interpreters are culturally situated; their interpretations
are anchored in and take the concrete, everyday lived experiences of
their interpretive community seriously; hence the readings themselves are cultural products.

Reading through the lens of my African/Cameroonian social location, I contended that both the story of the loving neighbor and the
book of Esther have high relevance and applicability to multivalent
situations beyond their cultural context. As a result, I claimed both
texts speak to the realities of Cameroonian/African social, cultural
backgrounds. The historical circumstances or social relations out of
which both stories emerge differ greatly from Cameroon's sociopolitical and cultural conditions. Accordingly, to make sense of both
stories within Cameroon's cultural settings, it is vital to recontextu-
alize the narratives within an African worldview and culture.

I showed that in Luke 10:25-37, the Samaritan's actions epitomize
the quintessential example of the dual mandate to love God and to
love our neighbor. The Samaritan's example of love for neighbor demonstrates that it is only selfless, risky, and sometimes financially costly
love that can turn prejudice on its head. Working from the premise

that discrimination and xenophobia are global phenomena, I illustrate how the Jewish/Samaritan conflict correlates with present-day concrete realities of intra-ethnic and inter-ethnic biases and conflicts in the Ngoketunjia Division. Like the ancient Jewish/Samaritan conflicts, the intense hatred among ethnic groups in the Ngoketunjia Division is also based on social markers such as ethnicity, religion, regional origin, tribal language, socioeconomic status, and gender. These social markers provide the historical underpinnings of interpersonal relationships in Cameroon as a whole. It is also the quintessential barrier to social inclusion.

The various ethnic groups in Ngoketunjia have equally promoted a culture of looking the other way rather than supporting religious-ethnic outsiders being targeted by prejudice. The loving neighbor story underlines that membership in one's cultural group should not inhibit radical hospitality toward members of the out group. Very often, the stereotypes we form about groups of people different from us are biased and inaccurate.

In a nutshell, if the ethnic groups in Ngoketunjia heed Jesus' advice to "go and do likewise" (Luke 10:37), that is, to emulate the risky love exemplified by the Samaritan, they too will be able to transcend social, ethnic, and religious boundaries. Jesus sets the Samaritan up as the moral exemplar at the most liberating and transformative moment of the story, when the lawyer concedes the Samaritan Other related ethically toward the victim. The lawyer's response propelled Jesus' final appeal to emulate the Samaritan's highest level of hospitality. The Samaritan's selfless and radically inclusive generosity serves as a blueprint for all who want to follow his actions. His actions also function as a basis for introspection that compels the lawyer and readers to confront their prejudices, whether explicit or implicit.

As I intimated in the previous section, African women read the narrative in the book of Esther through the lens of historically specific structures of patriarchal domination. The story notably offers them the incentive to probe issues of gender justice and patriarchal power relations. Similar to the Persian Empire, patriarchal power relations are institutionalized and normalized in Cameroon. Cameroonian women equally experience multifaceted injustice due to gender, ethnicity, and class. I proposed the intersectional interpretive framework as a way of understanding and analyzing the complexity in the characterization of Vashti and Esther. I showed that the narrative of Esther undergirds patriarchal assumptions and gender relationships. I equally maintained that Esther is not merely a passive, submissive, acquiescing, and self-sacrificing woman. She resisted her subjugation by astutely playing the game of Persian court politics and, by so doing, challenged patriarchal gender norms, asserted her agency, and effected social change and transformation. Esther, therefore, represents not a static but a dynamic character. She undergoes significant changes as the story progresses. It is her vibrant personality that made her foil the impending genocide and persecution against the Jews. She represents the emancipatory possibility for African women who cannot overtly violate gender-role expectations or openly challenge core patriarchal principles as Vashti did. Esther, like African women, must work within the system to transform traditional social structures.

Strong and independent African women reading the book of Esther are energized by Vashti's assertive character to challenge and destabilize the gendered expectations placed on them. Vashti's insubordination and ultimate fate are that of all vulnerable and marginal women. Like Vashti, some African women are undeterred by the potential consequences of challenging dominant gender norms and expectations. Vashti's openly defiant character invigorates them with the courage to challenge patriarchal and religious social structures that reinforce and legitimize oppressive practices against women.

CONSIDERING THE WHOLE

- Have you read the story of the loving neighbor or the book of Esther from the perspective of your social location or cultural lens?

- What are some of the contextual variables informing and shaping your reading of the loving neighbor and Esther stories?

- How might the dynamic relationship between the biblical text and your context enable the loving neighbor and the Esther story to come alive in your contemporary context?

- Does your culture exclude anyone based on the demographic they represent? How might you work with your community to confront explicit or blatant prejudice?

SUGGESTIONS FOR FURTHER READING

Kanyoro, M. R. A. *Introducing Feminist Cultural Hermeneutics: An African Perspective.* Sheffield: Sheffield Academic Press, 2002.

Mbuvi, Andrew. "African Biblical Studies: An Introduction to an Emerging Discipline." *Currents in Biblical Research* 15 (2017): 149-78.

Mosala, Itumeleng J. "The Implications of the Text of Esther for African Women's Struggle for Liberation in South Africa." In *The Postcolonial Biblical Reader*, edited by Rasiah S. Sugirtharajah, 134-41. Malden, MA: Blackwell Publishing, 2006.

Ukpong, Justin S. "Rereading the Bible with African Eyes: Inculturation and Hermeneutics." *Journal of Theology for Southern Africa* 91 (1995): 3-14.

4

EUROPEAN AND EURO-AMERICAN APPROACHES

JUSTIN MARC SMITH

THIS CHAPTER COVERS THE FEATURES AND THEMES present in the dominant perspectives of Western European and North American interpretations of the Bible. Europe, Canada, and the United States of America represent roughly one billion people. To put this into some perspective, it has been estimated that the population of the entire planet has reached 7.8 billion. This means that Europe, Canada, and the United States together represent just about one-seventh of the world's population. While this seems like a significant amount, India and China alone account for approximately 2.7 billion people. It is safe to say that while Europe, Canada, and the United States account for a significant portion of the world's population, these regions represent a minority in relation to the overall population of the world. And yet this minority voice has come to dominate the way the Bible is read and interpreted. This perspective has come to be the major voice in terms of the perspectives and approaches used to read and interpret Scripture across cultural, social, economic, and racial contexts.

In some ways, this chapter is a departure from the other chapters in this book. This chapter seeks to de-center the role of standard European/Euro-American approaches. As we will see, these approaches have become the default. In many ways, the perspectives of Western Europe and North America are all too often viewed as the *only* way to read and interpret Scripture. This can be seen in many of the textbooks and volumes that are produced on biblical criticism and biblical interpretation. Even in one of the more widely accepted and standard texts on biblical criticism and interpretation, eight of the fourteen chapters are dedicated to methods and approaches that come directly from the Western intellectual tradition. Only two of the fourteen chapters examine approaches that take gender or socio-economic status into account.[1] Similarly, in another well-known and widely used book on the topic, only three of the eighteen chapters cover methodologies that connect specifically to the perspectives of women and people of color.[2] Some readers may not fully appreciate the issue here. Simply put, women and people of color represent the vast majority of the population of the world (and the growing majority of Christians). If the world is indeed the wide and diverse place that we know it to be, then the perspectives used to read and interpret Scripture *in* the world and *with* the world should be wide and varied as well. It needn't be either-or when talking about global or Euro-American scholarship; it can and should be both/and; no one perspective should dominate the discussion.

But there is a certain irony here. All of the authors of this current volume have either been trained in North America or within the larger scope of these standard approaches to reading Scripture. We are able to do the kind of work that we are seeking to do here because

---

[1]Steven L. McKenzie and Stephen R. Haynes, eds., *To Each Its Own Meaning: An Introduction to Biblical Criticisms and Their Application*, rev. and expanded ed. (Louisville, KY: Westminster John Knox, 1999).

[2]Joel B. Green, ed., *Hearing the New Testament: Strategies for Interpretation* (Grand Rapids, MI: Eerdmans, 2010), v-vi.

of that training. And yet, it is because of that training that we are able to see the strengths and challenges of the very approaches that we have been trained in and have used.

To make this a bit more personal, I would like to share an anecdote from my own time in seminary. One of the courses that I was required to take was a course on exegetical methods and practices. Exegesis is the practice of explaining or critically examining a text. The term is derived from the Greek word *exēgēsis*, which means to lead to or draw out a detailed explanation or interpretation.[3] On the first day of class the professor came in and declared that "this class should be called 'Exegetical Method and Practice' because there is *only one method* for doing exegesis." The point was that the historical-critical method (and its related approaches) was the *only* correct way to read and interpret the Bible.[4]

On its face, the idea that there is one and only one interpretation of Scripture, and that this can be ascertained with a very specific set of tools and methods, is very attractive. In fact, many of us have been taught that this is the case, and for many years the authors of this book felt the same way. But in time we have come to see that many different approaches are needed in order to tap into the depths of meaning of Scripture. Exegesis can be a good thing, and it is still preferred in many instances to eisegesis, or reading one's own perspective or ideas into the text. But certain exegetical approaches assume that one can read in such a way as to be completely and wholly objective. While some might find this kind of objectivity ideal, it is not actually possible (or even desirable) that a reader would be able to shake off their contexts in such a way as to read without some bias. To some extent, the purpose of this chapter is to alert the reader to the implicit biases

[3]Walter Bauer, *A Greek-English Lexicon of the New Testament and Other Early Christian Literature*, ed. Frederick W. Danker, 3rd ed. (Chicago: University of Chicago Press, 2000), 349.
[4]In order to avoid being repetitive, historical-critical method(s) (and its related approaches) will often be synonymous with the dominant approach in European/Euro-American interpretive methodologies.

(both positive and negative) of Western approaches to reading Scripture. In the end, we are not asking students and readers of this book to completely divest themselves of the realities of their contexts, but to better understand them and then to be open to reading Scripture with the perspectives and through the lives of others.

PRESENTING FEATURES AND THEMES IN STANDARD EURO-AMERICAN APPROACHES

One of the most dominant (if not *the* most dominant) cultural expressions of the Western European world was the advance of so-called scientific criticism into the realm of the study of history, religion, and theology. This advancement began in the Enlightenment Period (c. 1650–1780) and has continued in various ways to the current era. Painting with broad strokes, we might identify a few key developments from this period that came to influence scientific study as well as historical research. It is out of this period that what is now known as the scientific method developed. This approach to the world dictates that what we come to know about the world is derived from verifiable and repeatable experiments and careful observation.[5] This challenges the previous notions that what was authoritative and true was derived from the Bible and/or the authority of the church.

In some ways, the new scientific approaches could be seen by some to be an attack on the Bible and the church as a source of authority. However, this is not what was intended. Rather, the hope was that by using independent scientific methods, one could *verify* what is true about the world, Scripture, and God in a way that was free from the superstitious and uninformed ways of thinking from the past.[6] Simply put, the scientific method was expected to confirm theological ideas. This reliance on scientific methodologies and the resulting

---

[5]James D. G. Dunn, *Jesus Remembered,* Christianity in the Making, vol. 1 (Grand Rapids, MI: Eerdmans, 2003), 26.
[6]Dunn, *Jesus Remembered,* 26.

preferences for secular approaches to knowledge-building led to the modern era (c. 1780–1990s) and the application of these methodologies to the study of history, and by extension, the Bible. Four key presuppositions emerged from this era, and had (and continue to have) a profound influence on the study of history. (1) History is an objective discipline, and the "facts" of history can be observed and discovered just like scientific facts. (2) Historians/scholars/students can be objective in their study of these "facts." (3) Human reason is a sufficient tool (and perhaps the only tool) needed to sort out fact from falsehood. Finally, (4) the universe and the world are governed by certain, unquestionable, and God-given natural laws.[7] These laws govern everything that happens in the physical world, and likewise, whatever happens in history should conform to these laws as well.

The aftereffects of these presuppositions have typically moved in one or two major directions. The first (the "scientific approach") is to take these presuppositions very seriously and to read and reread Scripture through the lens of modern historical inquiry.[8] In this way, only the parts of the biblical texts that can be verified independently and that withstand rigorous scrutiny are deemed to be historically valid. One very straightforward example of this is the crucifixion of Jesus. While historians and biblical scholars alike debate the exact details of the event, it is widely accepted that the Roman prefect of Judea, Pontius Pilate, crucified Jesus of Nazareth. This is an accepted historical fact because non-Christian historians (Josephus, Suetonius, and Tacitus), writing at a time that was roughly contemporary to the time of Jesus, refer to the event. More recently, Pilate's existence has been confirmed through inscriptional evidence. So, the Gospels record that Jesus of Nazareth was crucified under Pontius Pilate, but other non-Christian sources record this, too, and there is archaeological evidence to support

---

[7]Points 1–4 are covered in Dunn, *Jesus Remembered*, 27-28.
[8]Here "scientific approach" and "ambivalent approach" are being used not in a technical sense and are not intended to be used pejoratively. The purpose is to simply demark these two different approaches.

the existence of Pilate. As a result, this part of the Jesus narrative is most likely historically accurate. However, since only Christian writers recorded the resurrection of Jesus, and since there is no independent, non-Christian verification of this event, many scholars doubt the historical validity of the bodily resurrection of Jesus of Nazareth.

If we look more concretely at the development of the field of biblical studies, we can see some other specific examples indicating this shift in perspective. For instance, if we look at the growth of the field around the study of Jesus as a historical figure, we see some interesting developments. One of the first major developments related to the historical study of Jesus came through the work of Hermann Reimarus (1694–1768). Reimarus sought to draw out the distinctions between how Jesus understood himself and his movement and how the disciples saw it. In this way, he was one of the first Western scholars to draw a distinction between the Jesus of the Gospel texts (written by Jesus' disciples/followers) and Jesus as a historical figure. Any part of the text that differed with what Jesus clearly said about himself was deemed *unhistorical*.

The next move in historical Jesus study came through the work of David Strauss (1801–1874). Strauss doubted the validity of the miracles recorded in the Gospels. The Western world was coming to appreciate and accept the understanding of the universal/scientific laws that govern the universe, which meant that everything that happens in the world should conform to these natural laws. This would include miracles. The way that Strauss sought to deal with the issue was to understand the miracles as "myth." Myth was understood to be "an expression or embodiment of an idea."[9] Strauss extended this idea of myth to all of the Gospels and saw them, *not* as historical (or straightforwardly historically relevant) documents, but as the ideas of the early believers in Jesus about Jesus himself.[10]

---

[9]Dunn, *Jesus Remembered*, 32.
[10]Dunn, *Jesus Remembered*, 32-33.

The final move in this era came with the work of William Wrede (1859–1906). Through an analysis of the text of the Gospel of Mark, Wrede determined that the Synoptic Gospels (Matthew, Mark, Luke) were inherently theological and not necessarily helpful for doing historical research. Wrede understood that the Synoptic Gospels "were not portrayals of Jesus as he was, but of Jesus as his disciples subsequently saw him."[11] In the end, Wrede questioned whether the Synoptic Gospels could realistically be used as history. For Wrede, either the Synoptics were historical (conforming to the methodologies of Western modernity) or they are theological documents. They could not be both. One can do history, and one can do theology, but they should be kept separate. It was not clear to Wrede that the Gospel writers had done a good job of keeping their theology separate from their historical reporting of the life and work of Jesus.

The work of these scholars can be summarized in the following ways: (1) There is a clear difference between who Jesus was (and as he saw himself) and how his disciples saw him. The disciples' understanding of Jesus was deemed unhistorical and had no place in understanding Jesus as a historical figure. (2) The miraculous in the Gospels was inherently fictional and not indicative of Jesus himself, but was indicative of what the disciples thought about Jesus. (3) The Gospels were far too theological to be used to reconstruct Jesus as a historical figure. One could engage the theology of the Gospels, but one could not use the Gospels as historical fact. In reflecting on the work of Reimarus, Strauss, and Wrede, the implications are obvious: any part of the biblical text that cannot be independently verified is open to intense scrutiny and/or rejection.

The second approach (the "ambivalent approach") has been taken up by many Christians in the current context. This approach has been to reject (or at times ignore) the conclusions of biblical scholarship, while at the same time using the exegetical methodologies developed

---

[11]Dunn, *Jesus Remembered*, 50. See William Wrede, *The Messianic Secret* (Cambridge: Clark, 1971).

in the modern era to read and interpret Scripture.[12] The results have been mixed, at best. Embedded in this approach has been a holdover notion that one's reading of Scripture can be purely objective and that social location (race, gender, educational level, economic status, health concerns, etc.) need not have any bearing on reading the text. In other words, much like the presuppositions of the Enlightenment, exegesis can be done so that universal truths about God, humanity, and the world can be uncovered and understood.[13] These truths would be "applicable to people at all times and in all places."[14] The irony here is that the attempt to interpret the biblical texts using the methodologies of modernity, while rejecting the conclusions brought from that very enterprise, puts many Christians on a theological collision course: either accept the findings of these approaches to Scripture or find another way of reading and interpreting. Fundamentally, the kinds of questions we ask dictate the kinds of answers we get. If we are going to seek to read Scripture through the lenses and methodologies of the Western European cultural context, then we have to be willing to accept the outcomes.

The outcomes of these approaches may have become further complicated by the advent of postmodernity and its methodologies to some degree. Postmodern approaches tend to question the validity of universal meaning and application, and in this way differ substantially with the aims and outcomes of modernist approaches.[15] Standard North American and Western European approaches to reading and interpreting the biblical texts have tended to move in one of two

---

[12]Don Thorsen and Keith H. Reeves, *What Christians Believe About the Bible: A Concise Guide for Students* (Grand Rapids, MI: Baker Academic, 2012), 15.

[13]Thorsen and Reeves, *What Christians Believe*, 15.

[14]Thorsen and Reeves, *What Christians Believe*, 15.

[15]There is probably too much for us to unpack with postmodernism. The purpose here is just to mention it as a significant cultural shift and, in particular, to note the effect it has had on American and European worldviews. See Jean-Francois Lyotard, *The Postmodern Condition: A Report on Knowledge*, Theory and History of Literature 10 (Manchester, UK: Manchester University Press, 1984), 72. For a helpful introduction to postmodernism, see Linda Hutcheon, ed., *A Postmodern Reader*, 2nd ed. (Albany: SUNY Press, 1993).

opposite directions.[16] Functionally, either one adheres strictly to the findings of historical inquiry and is left with "holes" in the biblical account (the scientific approach), or one adheres less strictly, keeps the whole of the text intact, but leaves oneself open to questions of historical accuracy (the ambivalent approach). Thus, in one direction we have academic, historical, and "scientific" rigor, and in the other direction we have the adoption of the methodologies of modern research, but they are tempered with the understanding of Scripture as being the divine Word of God, and all interpretations must remain consistent with the theological realities of God.

One of the overarching aims of the ambivalent approach, especially within Christian circles, has been to attempt to find a single and universal meaning for each and every passage of Scripture. The potential advantage here is to find (eventually, and hopefully once and for all) the one true meaning of any given passage. This would allow for some sense of a universal interpretation and application. The thought here is that if God intended humanity to have Scripture, and if God intended Scripture to be God's Word to humanity, there must be a single meaning that all humanity can accept. If there is *not* one meaning for all people in all places and in all times, then what is the point? A purely objective approach, one grounded in the rigor of Enlightenment and scientific methods, would seem to have the best chance to find such a universal meaning and interpretation. The potential challenge here is in the reliance (or overreliance) on human reason and wisdom in the process of finding a single, universal biblical truth. Humans are fantastically talented beings, but we have our limitations, and placing our interpretive understanding squarely in the hands of human reason is both challenging and dangerous. As Dunn has argued, "Critical scholarship is never critical enough unless and until it is also self-critical and with equal vigour."[17]

---

[16]Postmodernism might represent another direction, especially in its rejection of metanarratives. See Lyotard, *Postmodern Condition*, 72.
[17]Dunn, *Jesus Remembered*, 34.

In thinking about the historical development that I have outlined, a few observations emerge. (1) The excitement of Enlightenment thinking and modernist approaches led to a certain confidence in the human ability to read and interpret biblical texts objectively. While the desire for objectivity is admirable, it is rarely (if ever) achievable. (2) As biblical scholars in the West (Europe and later North America) began to employ these new scientific approaches to reading the text, the outcomes challenged traditional readings of the text and further (at points) estranged biblical studies from traditional or classical theologies of the church. Finally, (3) the interaction with scientific approaches to Scripture have included an embracing of these approaches as well as an ambivalence toward them. In either instance, this methodology has dominated biblical studies (both academic and otherwise) in the European and North American context and continues to shape how the biblical texts are read.

STOP AND THINK

- What do you perceive are some of the strengths and weaknesses of Enlightenment approaches to reading, studying, and interpreting Scripture?

- What are the biases that standard Euro-American approaches bring to the reading of Scripture? Do you share any of them? If so, which ones?

READING TEXTS

Given what we have said about Western European and Northern American perspectives, what does this approach look like in practice? How do rationalistic/scientific and/or historical approaches produce a specific reading or interpretation of Scripture? Let's examine two different passages: one from the Christian Scriptures (Luke 10:25-37,

the parable of the loving neighbor) and one from the Hebrew Bible
(2 Samuel 11:1-27, David and Bathsheba).[18]

The Parable of the Loving Neighbor (Luke 10:25-37)

It is probably not too great a stretch to say that the parable of the
loving neighbor is the most well-known parable of Jesus next to the
parable of the prodigal son (Luke 15:11-32). In the previous chapter
(Luke 9:51-56), Jesus has begun his travels to Jerusalem, where he will
eventually be arrested and crucified. As part of his move toward Jerusalem, Jesus sends out messengers to announce his arrival to various
towns and villages along the way. At one point, the messengers come
to a Samaritan village and announce that Jesus is coming. However,
Jesus is rejected when the Samaritans find out he is on the way to
Jerusalem and not specifically (or only) to them. As Jesus continues
to Jerusalem, he sends out seventy disciples in pairs (Luke 10:1-12)
with the mission of preparing the way for Jesus himself, and in turn
seeking out hospitality for both Jesus and the disciples. On the return
of the seventy and their report of positive progress (Luke 10:17-20),
Jesus rejoices at the faith of the disciples and the revelation of God's
power to them (Luke 10:21-24).

It is at this precise moment, after Jesus has just thanked God for
revealing God's self to this group of disciples, that an expert in the law
stands up and asks, "What must I do to inherit eternal life?" (Luke 10:25).
The issues being raised here are complex, but one way to understand
the legal expert's question is simply this: "How can I be sure I'll be
saved in the final resurrection?"[19] Jesus' response is to draw the expert
into the content of the text of the law (Luke 10:26). Given the expert's
response about loving God and loving neighbors, it seems probable
that Jesus was intending to draw him into this basic reality of living,
and one that was well-articulated in the daily recitations of

---

[18]All of the scholars referenced in this section are from the Western European or North American context.

[19]Darrell L. Bock, *Luke 9:51–24:53*, BECNT (Grand Rapids, MI: Baker Academic, 1996), 1023.

Deuteronomy 6:5 and in the related actions of loving one's neighbors in Leviticus 19:18. This connecting of the commands to love God and love neighbors is a hallmark of Jewish understanding and devotion.[20] Jesus commends the expert for his answer (Luke 10:28), but the legal expert wants to be certain to have the demands to love others clarified (Luke 10:29). He wants to know what Jesus means here. What are the limits to love? How does Jesus understand the parameters of love? The expert may be seeking to find what the lower limit (the least amount) of love is.

Jesus responds with a parable about a man who is beaten, robbed, and left for dead on the dangerous road from Jerusalem to Jericho (Luke 10:30). Two prominent legal experts (a priest and a Levite) pass by and do nothing to help this beaten and nearly dead man (Luke 10:31). It is not those trained in a deeper understanding of the mercies of the law and love that attend to the needs of this broken man as one of their own. No, it is the Samaritan, the enemy and outsider, who offers mercy and first aid. He attends to the needs of the man; he delivers him to a place where he can be kept safe and receive care; and he offers to pay for two days of care up front with a promise to pay whatever costs that have accrued when he returns (Luke 10:34-35). When asked who the neighbor in this parable was, the legal expert responds, "the one who showed mercy" (Luke 10:37).

So, what do we make of this parable? One of the strengths of the standard Euro-American approach is the unpacking of the first-century historical and cultural factors at play here, and there are several issues to unpack. The first is the context. In the previous chapter (Luke 9:51-56), Jesus and his group have been rejected by a Samaritan village. Given the discussion of the Jewish/Samaritan tensions in the previous chapters of this book, I will simply say this: the rejection of Jesus by Samaritans should come as no surprise. The long-standing disagreement between Samaritans and Jews over which

---

[20]Bock, *Luke 9:51–24:53*, 1025-26.

group was the true representation of God's people, as well as religious and political tensions, made Jesus' rejection likely. Simply put: Jews and Samaritans were enemies (when Jesus is rejected by the Samaritans in Luke 9:54, the disciples ask Jesus if he wants them "to command fire to come down from heaven and consume" the village; it is no better in John 4:9; 8:48).[21] The larger context of Jewish/Samaritan relations and the rejection of Jesus by a Samaritan village presents the Samaritan as the most unlikely example of mercy in the parable.

Second, we can examine some of the historical realities of the parable. It should be remembered here that the parable is just that: a parable. It is a fictional narrative designed to illustrate a larger point or reality about the kingdom of God. This is not an anecdote couched in some specific and actual historical reality. Nonetheless, there are historical elements to the narrative. The parable is set on the long, dangerous, and often treacherous road from Jerusalem to Jericho. The hazardous reputation of this road was well-known even in the times before Jesus. It was unsafe. The presence of travelers on this road was not uncommon, and it may well be the case that in this period Jericho had begun to function as a suburb for Jerusalem, with a large population of priests and others associated with the functions of the temple in Jerusalem living in Jericho.[22] Given that the two legal experts in the parable are going from Jerusalem to Jericho, it would seem more than likely that they are returning home after serving in an official capacity, and concerns about becoming impure or defiled for touching a dead body (Leviticus 21:1-3) are not at play here (see Leviticus 19:16 for the suggestion that aid could be given legally).[23] But the reality is that

---

[21]James R. Edwards, *The Gospel According to Luke*, PNTC (Grand Rapids, MI: Eerdmans, 2015), 322.

[22]John T. Carroll, *Luke: A Commentary*, New Testament Library (Louisville, KY: Westminster John Knox, 2012), 245.

[23]Bock, *Luke 9:51–24:53*, 1030. One of the hallmarks of Euro-American readings is a direct engagement with the original languages. This is especially true of academic readings of the text. In this case, the movement toward Jericho and away from Jerusalem is indicated by the Greek verb *katabainō*, which means to go down. This verb suggests that the travelers in this narrative are likely traveling northeast from Jerusalem to Jericho but traveling downward in elevation.

Jesus gives no rationale for the refusal of the priest or Levite to offer help. The desire to avoid danger or defilement could be implied, but these reasons are not stated.

Third, we can assess the point of the parable. Given the context of the parable and the desire of the legal expert to "justify" himself, we might ask again why the expert asks Jesus who his neighbor is (Luke 10:29). The connection to "eternal life" and justification points to the desire on the part of the lawyer to establish the minimum amount of care and concern needed to be compliant to the law. There is a sense in which the question seeks to establish a boundary for care and concern. The response on the part of Jesus through the parable is to push the boundaries of care and concern to their most uncomfortable limits. By portraying the hated and despised Samaritan as the one who shows mercy to the broken and beaten Jew, Jesus holds up the outsider, and even the enemy, as the model of love and mercy. This is contrasted with the unloving and unmerciful response of the legal experts in the parable. If the question is "Who is my neighbor?" then the answer is a resounding, "Everyone, including your most hated enemy!" Even the legal expert can recognize the example of the Samaritan and acknowledge that the one who is a neighbor is the one who demonstrates mercy (Luke 10:37). It is at this point that Jesus instructs him to go and model this radical expression of love and compassion.

Finally, from the standard Euro-American perspective, we can ask, What does this mean in the current context? How do we apply this today, and what is the one universal meaning of this passage? It would seem that in the passage Luke presents Jesus as one who envisions a radical love and mercy. This love and mercy extends the call to love one's neighbors past the traditional boundaries of family friends and immediate community to those at the most extreme edges and margins. To be a loving neighbor means to love those we find it hard to love. We are called to show mercy to those we find to be the most unworthy of mercy. We are called to cross ethnic and racial boundaries to meet all with love and grace. The legal expert joins the call to love God with the call to love neighbors (Luke 10:27), and in so doing he has articulated the idea that one cannot love God and be unloving and unmerciful to others. The legal expert's concern, and likely the concern for many of us, is who should be considered in the category of neighbor. Jesus' response is to challenge him with an expanded definition of neighbor, and one that includes enemies. This definition pushes both the legal expert and the modern reader in the direction of transformative and life-changing expressions of love for all.

David and Bathsheba (2 Samuel 11:1-27)

As the narrative opens, the reader finds that it is spring, and the Israelites have gone out to war with the Ammonites (2 Samuel 11:1). David has sent Joab, his most capable general, out to battle and "David [has] remained at Jerusalem" (2 Samuel 11:1). One afternoon, David gets up from his couch and wanders around on the roof of his house where he sees a beautiful woman bathing some distance away. He sends his emissaries to find out who the woman is (2 Samuel 11:2-3). When he finds out that the woman is Bathsheba, wife of Uriah the Hittite (one of David's best soldiers), David sends for her, has sexual relations with her, and sends her away (2 Samuel 11:3-4). A short time later, David finds out that Bathsheba is pregnant with his child (2 Samuel 11:5). David sends for Uriah and tries multiple times to entice him to sleep with Bathsheba so that David can cover up the pregnancy (2 Samuel 11:6-13). When this fails, David orders Joab (through a sealed letter carried by Uriah!) to place Uriah in the thick of the fighting and then withdraw his troops so that Uriah will be killed (2 Samuel 11:14-25). After Bathsheba is done mourning the death of her husband, David makes her his wife (2 Samuel 11:26-27a).

It is not difficult to see the issues with this narrative: David is engaged with adultery, murder, collusion, and the list goes on. Walter Brueggemann puts it this way:

It is the abrupt transition from a life under blessing to a life under curse. It is the intrusion of a sin into the life of David (and Israel) that cuts so sharply that it rivals in power the "original" act of Adam and Eve. The story is so massive and penetrating that it almost defies our capacity to interpret. Every effort fails before the subject itself, no doubt the way interpretation fails all great art.[24]

Here the reader/interpreter is forced to understand at a deeper level how it is that David, "a man after his [God's] own heart" (1 Samuel 13:14), could perpetrate such a heinous act. Does this say something about God? What does this say about what it means to be "a man after his [God's] own heart"? Perhaps some of the solution to the narrative lies in the reality of sexual temptation and desire that is so much a part of the human experience.

As European scholar Hans Hertzberg has pointed out, the interaction of David and Bathsheba is facilitated by her bathing in such a way that she might conceivably draw attention to herself.[25] The homes of the wealthy in Jerusalem would have "included multiple courtyards containing kitchens, wells, baths, and even shade trees."[26] Presumably, homes closer to the residence of David would have been of this higher social location. Bathsheba might well have been washing in a bath in one of the courtyards of her home. This would have put her within the proximity of the gaze of David, whose residence was likely larger and taller than the others. When David went out on the roof of his home in the afternoon (2 Samuel 11:2), it was likely not difficult for him to see Bathsheba. Some commentators have even suggested that blame should be placed on Bathsheba (at least in part) for bathing so publicly and that attracting male attention might have been the reason for doing so.[27] In short, they argue, it is not entirely

---

[24]Walter Brueggemann, *First and Second Samuel*, Interpretation (Louisville, KY: John Knox Press, 1990), 272.

[25]Hans Wilhelm Hertzberg, *I and II Samuel: A Commentary*, Old Testament Library (Philadelphia: The Westminster Press, 1974), 309.

[26]Tony W. Cartledge, *1 and 2 Samuel*, Smyth & Helwys Bible Commentary (Macon, GA: Smyth & Helwys, 2001), 498.

[27]Hertzberg, *I and II Samuel*, 309.

clear that Bathsheba is an unwitting victim; rather, she may have been at least partially willing to engage in this adulterous behavior.[28] Other scholars have suggested that the strange line "now she was purifying herself after her period" (2 Samuel 11:4) may have been included to indicate that Bathsheba was at or near a particularly fertile time and that biological reality would not have been lost on her. In this case, the resulting pregnancy would not have been a shock to her.

In the estimation of yet other Euro-American interpreters, David's sin and lust is perhaps mitigated in part by the cooperation of Bathsheba. The writer of the text of 2 Samuel seems to be less willing to absolve David of his guilt. Once this terrible series of events has come to an end, the author concludes in 2 Samuel 11:27b, "But the thing that David had done displeased the LORD." David's cunning and treachery do not end with his sexual relations with Bathsheba. David tries to draw Uriah into the plot to cover up the unwanted and inconvenient pregnancy of 2 Samuel 11:5. David summons Uriah, one of David's most trusted soldiers and a member of the "Thirty" (2 Samuel 23:8-39), and attempts to encourage him to go home and sleep with Bathsheba. Out of duty to his fellow soldiers who remain in battle and away from their wives and families, Uriah refuses. David then tries to get Uriah drunk in order to entice him to go home to Bathsheba (2 Samuel 11:6-13). Finally rebuffed, David seeks to have Uriah killed in battle (2 Samuel 11:14-25).

With the deed done, the reader is left to determine what to make of David. As the rest of the narrative unfolds, we find that God is not pleased with David and that David is ultimately punished (2 Samuel 12:1-23), with David first being condemned by the prophet Nathan, and with the child of David and Bathsheba eventually dying (2 Samuel 12:15b-23). Given the standard Euro-American approach employed here, the meaning of the text is fixed and clear. David sins

---

[28]Robert Barron, 2 *Samuel*, Brazos Theological Commentary on the Bible (Grand Rapids, MI: Brazos Press, 2015), 99.

by coveting Uriah's wife; David sins by committing adultery with her; Bathsheba is not without fault here as she goes to the king and has relations with him. Finally, David compounds his sin, first by trying to cover up Bathsheba's pregnancy, then by trying to coerce Uriah into having sex with his wife. When neither ploy works, he orders Uriah's death. Lust, adultery, dishonesty, coercion, and murder—David manages to commit many of the most recognized and reviled sins all in one series of actions. David is punished and yet, presumably, remains "a man after his [God's] own heart." From the standard Euro-American perspective, the message and meaning are clear: sin is wrong, but God can forgive even the most egregious of sins. Yet some important questions and concerns remain.

REFLECTING ON THE TEXTS

- Are standard Western European/North American approaches helpful here? Why or why not?

- How might we experience the parable of the loving neighbor if we read it through the eyes of the Samaritan?

- Is there anything that troubles you about how the narrative of David and Bathsheba is being interpreted here?

- How might this text be experienced differently if we read it from the perspective of Bathsheba? How might we understand this text differently if we considered the role of power in the narrative (i.e., who has power, who doesn't)?

CONCLUDING THOUGHTS

One of the challenges inherent in this methodology is the notion that there can be (and must be) one and only one right interpretation for a given text. This assertion would seem to be the byproduct of the use of modern historical methodologies on the biblical text while also rejecting the outcomes of many of those historical methodologies. The presupposition that there must be only one valid interpretation for a given biblical text is at its core a defense against interpretations that potentially challenge the historical accuracy of the biblical text. The challenge to the historicity of the biblical text was a natural consequence of the use of critical methodologies to read and interpret Scripture. If one is going to treat the Bible as a historical artifact, then one should expect it to conform to the expectations of history. The desire of standard Euro-American interpreters to use historical methodologies to arrive at a universal meaning for the text could be seen as an attempt to use history to transcend history. It is debatable whether this is completely possible. After all, as previously mentioned, the kinds of questions we ask dictate the kinds of answers we uncover.

Another potential challenge to this methodology lies in the assumption that the authoritative interpretation addresses the experiences and social locations of all readers. Are we to assume that Western European and North American approaches, which are couched in the principles of the Enlightenment and modernity, are to be adopted by all? Can we imagine that there might be some in the world who are not shaped by these philosophical and intellectual traditions? And if there are those who are not influenced by these principles, are we to suggest that they must understand and adopt these principles (which many in the West are currently wrestling with) in order to come to the one correct understanding of the biblical texts? Furthermore, are we to suggest that Western methodologies contain the best and ultimately only answer to understanding Scripture? I am not sure that most conscientious interpreters of Scripture would want to make many or most of those claims. But the unfortunate reality is that if we try to assert one universal reading of Scripture, we are forced to deal with the cultural, philosophical, and intellectual traditions that are producing that interpretation.

Thinking more concretely about the biblical passages discussed above, there are some rather troubling conclusions reached by many scholars in the West. In the narrative of David and Bathsheba (2 Samuel 11:1-27), most commentators and scholars read the narrative to produce a depiction of Bathsheba as culpable in the act of adultery. In one sense, many commentators seem to think that the adage "it takes two to tango" applies here. There is something in the very common and yet seductive act of bathing for which Bathsheba should be held accountable. She should have known that David could see her bathing, in the privacy of her own home, and she should have taken the appropriate steps to avoid a certain exhibitionist flair. Certainly, David is responsible for his actions, but so is Bathsheba. This rings as problematic, since nowhere does the narrative suggest any attempt of seduction on the part of Bathsheba. Are we to believe that she, in her feminine form, is naturally seductive and thus must take extra care not to tempt any man who might lay eyes on her? It would appear that this interpretive tradition stylizes Bathsheba, and perhaps women on the whole, as naturally temptresses who must monitor themselves for the sake of men. This is not helpful.

Even more troubling in the common Euro-American reading of this narrative is the lack of acknowledgment about what happens to Bathsheba. There is a certain reticence to label the event as sexual assault, even rape, on the part of David. Rarely is it discussed that when Bathsheba was "sent" for by David, and she "came" to him, and he "lay" with her, this whole matrix of interaction is couched within the reality of power and domination.[29] Yes, Bathsheba comes to David, but what choice did she have? Was she in a position to refuse the king? This is expressly a narrative of sexual power and sexual violence, and to silence the implication of sexual violence in the text is to silence the voices of those who have and continue to experience sexual violence in our own communities. Brueggemann, in his interpretation of these events and the condemnation of David by Nathan, states, "With the

---

[29]It should be pointed out that the passage includes the Hebrew phrase "and he took her" for the NRSV's more benign "to get." As 1 Samuel 8 promised, the king would be fundamentally a "taker." This comes to pass in the 2 Samuel 11 narrative.

words 'lie' and 'took,' however, there is also an accusation of rape. . . . This is a tale of cynicism, selfishness, destruction and greed."[30]

Similarly, in the parable of the loving neighbor (Luke 10:25-37), it is often acknowledged that the point of the parable is to manifest radical love and mercy to all regardless of race, culture, or ethnicity. While this is helpful, when told from the perspective of power and privilege it masks the truly difficult and dangerous reality of this call on the part of Jesus. Rarely is the parable viewed from the perspective of the Samaritan. Rarely is the parable viewed through the reality of what it might have been like to be a Samaritan in a doubly dangerous space. The road to Jericho was unsafe for Jews—in a Jewish region! How much more unsafe would it have been for the Samaritan to be on a perilous road in a space that is hostile to him simply because he was who he was: a Samaritan? What about the fear and concern of trying to do the merciful and loving thing by taking this broken and beaten Jewish man to an inn for care? How would the Samaritan have been received? Those in positions of power and privilege are able to talk about crossing the lines of race, culture, and social location in a way that tends to be safe. But it takes those who live and reside daily in these unsafe spaces to speak a new, resounding, and powerful truth into the reality of what it means to love and show mercy from the outside and from the margins.

I do not want to leave this chapter on a negative note. I recognize the tension here. On the one hand, all of the contributors to the book have benefited greatly from the insights of standard Euro-American approaches to reading Scripture. For most of us, the historical-critical approaches discussed in this chapter have formed the backbone of our education and our readings of the text. These approaches are important and enlightening. They should be celebrated for the way they have moved the discoveries within biblical studies forward. The perspectives of standard Western European and North American

---

[30]Walter Brueggemann, *First and Second Samuel*, 280.

interpreters have added immense value to the study and interpretation of Scripture. These approaches have sought to include intellect and reason in the process of interpretation. The rejection of superstitious and unfounded analyses has been helpful. Because of these viewpoints, we better understand the history and culture of the world of the biblical text. This knowledge has enabled us to read Scripture with more clarity, depth, and accuracy. As mentioned at the outset, it is in using many of these techniques that we can now see that there is a problem in allowing one approach to become the dominant voice for reading and interpreting. We recognize the need to de-center any one approach. As we embrace the plethora of readings, including the standard Western readings, we as interpreters are better equipped to ask new questions and to seek new answers that no single approach can address. We feel that making new discoveries and coming to new realizations is always exciting, challenging, and beneficial.

CONSIDERING THE WHOLE

- How would you summarize the content of this chapter in a few sentences?

- What questions has this chapter helped to answer? What questions are left unanswered?

SUGGESTIONS FOR FURTHER READING

Beilby, James K., and Paul Rhodes Eddy, eds. *The Historical Jesus: Five Views*. Downers Grove, IL: IVP Academic, 2009.

De La Torre, Miguel. *Reading the Bible from the Margins*. Maryknoll, NY: Orbis Books, 2002.

McCaulley, Esau. *Reading While Black: African American Biblical Interpretation as an Exercise in Hope*. Downers Grove, IL: IVP Academic, 2020.

McKenzie, Steven L., and Stephen R. Haynes, eds. *To Each Its Own Meaning: An Introduction to Biblical Criticisms and Their Application*, rev. and expanded ed. Louisville, KY: Westminster John Knox, 1999.

Reid, Barbara E. *Taking Up the Cross: New Testament Interpretation Through Latina and Feminist Eyes*, rev. ed. Minneapolis: Fortress, 2007.

5

ASIAN APPROACHES

KIRSTEN SONKYO OH

READING THE BIBLE AND INTERPRETING what it means has been a long cyclical process of studying, discerning, absorbing, and applying the Bible in both personal and communal ways. Countless volumes have been and will continue to be written on biblical hermeneutics, or the methods and principles of interpreting and discerning the meaning behind the various texts within the Bible. Biblical reading and studying were largely a male and Euro-American enterprise during the colonial years from the early nineteenth century and post-Enlightenment eras on the Asian continent. Since the mid-1970s, a shift in biblical interpretation emerged through the developmental progressions of reading the Bible not only through literary criticism, which took the various genres of the Scripture into account, but also by engaging cultural criticism. This integration of cultural studies with classical biblical hermeneutics broke open a broad continuum of multivalent interpretive perspectives. One stream of these approaches is Asian biblical hermeneutics.

As we approach Asian biblical hermeneutics, the first question to answer is, What is Asia? Geographically, Asia remains the largest continent in the world and includes numerous countries within East Asia, South Asia, Southeast Asia, and Russia, with a land mass covering over thirty percent of the earth's terrain and including over half of the population of the world. According to Rasiah Sugirtharajah, this large mass of countries was named "Asia" from the Chinese character *yaxiya*, or "inferior," on a map in 1584 by Matteo Ricci, an Italian Jesuit priest. "Asia" was simply a transliteration of China's self-perception of being the central nation surrounded by land and people who are "inferior" or "foreign" to China.[1] At the time, Asia referred to a vast continent that in plural form included four Asias: "West Asia (the Arab world), Central Asia (republics of the former Soviet Union), East Asia (extending to the Western Pacific nations), and South Asia (sub-Himalayan countries)."[2] In this chapter, Asia is used mostly in reference to East (China, Japan, Korea, Mongolia, and Taiwan), Southeast (Brunei, Cambodia, Indonesia, Laos, Malaysia, Philippines, Singapore, Thailand, Vietnam, etc.), and South (the Indian subcontinent) Asia, concurrent to the contemporary use of the term.[3] Needless to say, the sense of inferior versus superior has been jettisoned in the current use of the term.

The complexity of Asia as a geographical idea is analogous to Asian readings of the Bible. The transmission of the Bible to Asia and the subsequent reading of the text resonated at first with Buddhist, Hindu, and Confucian teachings. This resonance helped further prop up some systems of power and oppression. For instance, "the Confucianist ethic of nation before family and family before self, with the success of the self being bound to the economic prosperity of the

---

[1]R. S. Sugirtharajah, *The Bible and Asia: From the Pre-Christian Era to the Postcolonial Age* (Cambridge, MA: Harvard University Press, 2013), 2. There are other accounts of "Asia" having Greek etymology, meaning "sunrise."

[2]R. S. Sugirtharajah, ed., *Still at the Margins: Biblical Scholarship Fifteen Years After Voices from the Margin* (New York: T&T Clark, 2008), 3.

[3]Central and Eastern Asia are still in use to describe the subregions of the Middle East and southern part of Eastern Europe geographically, but in terms of the cultural or geopolitical scope, Asia is divided into the three subregions described here.

nation" was coupled with the Protestant work ethic that propelled capitalistic ventures and productions.[4] At the same time, the Bible was also read to liberate the subjugation from these systems of power as an answer to God's call for justice.

Since Asia itself is varied and complex, it will be important to first introduce (in broad brushstrokes) colonial biblical readings in Asia, followed by various ethnic, cultural, contextual, and postcolonial readings of the Bible, both past and present. In the background to this particular reading is the inevitable struggle of many Asian biblical scholars to liberate the Bible from its colonial roots and contextualize it within the Asian social location. This introductory chapter to reading the Bible through Asian eyes, then, demonstrates the power of various ethnicities within Asia to contextually partake in and disseminate interpretations of the Bible.

PRESENTING FEATURES AND THEMES
IN ASIAN APPROACHES

The apostle Thomas brought Christianity to India in 52 CE, according to church tradition, and Christianity took root in Asia more than a millennium before the various efforts of European and North American missionaries.[5] However, the introduction of the translated biblical texts and the concurrent interpretation of those texts in Asian languages was mostly recognized by the Asian audience as part of the Western missionary movement of the sixteenth through the twentieth centuries. Christianity in Asia, thereby, was generally known as a "Western religion."

---

[4]Stephen Chin Ming Lim, "The Impe(/a)rative of Dialogue in Asian Hermeneutics Within the Modern/Colonial World System: Renegotiating Biblical Pasts for Planetary Futures," *Biblical Interpretation* 25, no. 5 (2017): 673.

[5]Centuries later, the Church of the East (Nestorians from Persia) brought parts of the Bible and translated them into Chinese during the Tang dynasty (618–907 CE). It was noted by Arab traders that the Chinese emperor during a part of this dynasty knew the major narratives of the Bible, including the stories of Jesus, Moses, Noah, and some prophets. Cf. Samuel H. Moffett, *A History of Christianity in Asia*, 1st ed., 2 vols., American Society of Missiology Series 2 (San Francisco: HarperSanFrancisco, 1992), 25-36, 288-95.

As such, biblical interpretation from the colonial era in Asia was a production of Euro-American missionaries and their sending institutions. These colonial interpretations dominated the optics of biblical understanding in Asia. Such interpreting and translating of Scripture reflected a race, culture, language, and class bias that superimposed higher (colonizer) knowledge on what was presumed a lower (colonized) understanding of religious morality by most Bible translators and missionaries from that era. These interpretations presupposed a universality of the Bible's meaning without the contextuality of the text itself and of the religious, cultural, and ethnic traditions of each subjective place. What is more, biblical interpretation of this sort had tangible consequences. Stephen Lim, a Singaporean biblical scholar, summarizes, "The arrival of the Bible in many Asian nations often ended in violent conflicts with local religions and traditions."[6]

This colonial biblical understanding was most profound in the subcontinent of India because of its layered history with the arrival of European trading companies in the late sixteenth century and the establishment of British rule under Queen Victoria in 1858. Along with British rule came the wide introduction of the Bible and its interpretation. According to Sugirtharajah, Indian scholars wrestled with these interpretations in order to produce a nuanced biblical usage and understanding. Sugirtharajah's survey of Asian biblical interpretation with origins from the South Asian colonial era yields three categories of particular Asian reading of Scripture: Orientalist, Anglicist, and Nativist.[7] These terms arose during the British colonial rule over India in the late eighteenth century and were used to describe British scholars who either favored Indian traditions and laws, British traditions and law, or the vernacular traditions, respectively. These broad categories were interposed between readers and the Bible

---

[6]Lim, "Impe(/a)rative of Dialogue in Asian Hermeneutics," 664.
[7]R. S. Sugirtharajah, *Asian Biblical Hermeneutics and Postcolonialism: Contesting the Interpretations*, Bible & Liberation Series (Maryknoll, NY: Orbis Books, 1998).

by the missionaries from the West and influenced most Asian countries' experiences with the Bible.

Orientalist. The term *Orientalist* first was used in the late eighteenth century for English scholars who favored Asian or "oriental" texts, particularly during British colonial rule over India. Similarly, Orientalist biblical interpretation involved the advocacy of Western colonialists for the revival and promotion of the Eastern "ancient linguistic, philosophical, and religious heritage."[8] Orientalist interpreters of the Bible read original cultural texts with the aim of finding similarities between them and the Christian Scriptures. By comparing indigenous literary traditions, interpretive principles, and philosophical reasoning, Orientalists exegeted, understood, and taught the Bible. In Indian Orientalist biblical interpretation, the Bible "is seen as a medium, marginal to other mediations through which meanings can be obtained."[9] This interpretation couched biblical interpretation in mystical and allegorical meanings of transcendent knowledge.

Anglicist. The term *Anglicist* comes from the same colonial era as *Orientalist.* Anglicist biblical interpretation solely employed the critical methodologies of Western science, thinking, philosophy, and reasoning that were already integrated into the culture of the colonizing Westerner. In this model, all cultural contexts are jettisoned in favor of the original language and intent of the Bible. Anglicists believed that the one true original meaning of the Bible can only be discovered by the Western systematized review of the biblical texts' own context, language, and culture. These English colonizers emphasized British literature and European know-how as the "endorsement of Christian principles and an advancement of truth."[10] Through historical criticism using the modernist structure of grand narratives, Anglicists believed that universal, objective truths and normative meaning could be unearthed.

---

[8]Sugirtharajah, *Asian Biblical Hermeneutics*, 4.
[9]Sugirtharajah, *Asian Biblical Hermeneutics*, 7.
[10]Sugirtharajah, *Asian Biblical Hermeneutics*, 9.

Nativist. Nativist biblical interpretation insisted on the vernacular traditions of everyday storytelling. Biblical texts were interwoven with common, vernacular tales, anecdotes, and aphorisms to reconstitute biblical interpretations. For instance, they presented the story of Jesus in an "imaginative way of teaching the intricacies . . . to ordinary people through [familiar] musical accompaniments and recitations."[11] This so-called singable theology in Indian biblical interpretation used the vocabulary, concepts, and devotional writings of bhakti (worship or homage to a supreme deity) to introduce biblical stories.

Each of these three models of interpretation often contested, overlapped, and intersected with the other(s) in interpreting the Bible. While these models aimed to serve the people, they were nevertheless the colonizers' attempt to normalize a particular reading of the Bible. Inherent in these models of interpretation were the stereotyping and oversimplifying of indigenous groups. These essentializations of particular Asian cultures perpetuated the idea that a local culture is static and unchanging. The limitation of the elite Orientalist model was that it sought to resonate only traditional texts with the biblical text, and the limitation of the Nativist model was that it sought to indigenize the Bible in vernacular ways. Chinese American New Testament scholar Benny Liew asserts that biblical interpretation that is lodged in its primary particularity for the sake of "identity, authenticity, and legibility" will devolve not only because of its "exclusionary and ethnographical or colonial implication, but also because of its essentialist (mis)understanding of racial/ethnic identity."[12] That is, no group in itself remains monolithic, and no group in its entirety can be identified with one reductive perception of what that group's elite texts are and what that group may consider authentically vernacular.

---

[11]Sugirtharajah, *Asian Biblical Hermeneutics*, 13.
[12]Tat-Siong Benny Liew, *What Is Asian American Biblical Hermeneutics? Reading the New Testament*, Intersections: Asian and Pacific American Transcultural Studies (Honolulu: University of Hawai'i Press, 2008), 5.

In the last few decades, these missionary-era interpretations have given way to the development of biblical interpretation that has taken radical shifts. In particular, the historical-critical methodology that was prevalent in the Anglicist model exhibited inadequacies.[13] This methodology and its subsequent theology that perpetuated the power and privilege of the colonizer over against the colonized was comprehensively contested. Instead of the insistence that there exists only one true reading of the Bible, through the inclusion of literary criticism and cultural studies, biblical interpretation moved toward multiple interpretive possibilities. Such interdisciplinary engagements have given space for the emergence of contextual/global approaches. Simply put, contextual/global approaches consider the varied social locations within Asian contexts in their particular time and place and recognize God's preferential option for the poor and other marginalized groups.[14]

CONTEXTUAL BIBLICAL HERMENEUTICS

The diversity of Asia, a vast continent made up of manifold countries, languages, cultures, customs, traditions, and histories, even embedded within each country, cannot be clearer. In order not to essentialize Asia as a whole, it is paramount to broach Asian biblical hermeneutics by understanding the scope of its multilayered diversity, particularly its religious history. This multilayered approach has liberated biblical readings from a certain theological and interpretational myopia. This approach has demonstrated that biblical interpretations cannot be kept as the exclusive privilege of one normative

---

[13]Chloe Sun observes, "For Asian and Asian American biblical interpreters, the historical-critical methods proved insufficient to address the cultural and contextual particularities of the Asian and Asian American diaspora." Chloe Sun, "Recent Research on Asian and Asian American Hermeneutics Related to the Hebrew Bible," *Currents in Biblical Research* 17, no. 3 (2019): 241.

[14]Fernando F. Segovia, "Biblical Criticism and Postcolonial Studies: Toward a Postcolonial Optic," in *The Postcolonial Bible*, ed. R. S. Sugirtharajah (Sheffield: Sheffield Academic Press, 1998), 52-53.

reader, but diverse and dynamic biblical readings must be welcomed. Here is a historical and contextual example from Korea.

Christianity entered Korea by Korean traders who encountered Catholicism in China through Chinese scholars of Confucianism who were converted to Catholicism through the writings of Matteo Ricci.[15] At the time, Korea was known as the "Hermit Kingdom" due to its fear and subsequent resistance to any foreign influence. When Catholicism entered its borders through indigenous means, tremendous persecutions ensued, so much so that in 1866 over eight thousand Catholics were martyred by government orders. However, by the late nineteenth century, the borders of the country were open enough to have Protestantism enter the Korean peninsula through the effort of Korean converts and American missionaries.

This history of Korean Christianity gave rise to a mixture of Confucian, European, and American influences on biblical interpretations. Korean biblical scholar Tai Il Wang asserts that the biblical interpretations of the Euro-American missionaries were "consumed by the natural, scientific and rationalistic worldview of the West"; instead, he suggests that Korean Christians ought to interpret the text through "introvertedly partaking" of it so the text can become flesh and blood, the very being of the person.[16] In this personalized interpretation, scriptural narratives become the source of manna or food, not just for thought but for spiritual and emotional nourishment of empathy, comfort, and wisdom for the imbibers. Wang offers this "spiritual interpretation" as a corrective against the overly scientific and critical interpretation from the Enlightenment era. For example, "introvertedly partaking" the Bible for a lower-class, undereducated woman in a patriarchal system opens up two

---

[15]Ricci, a Jesuit missionary to China, brought mathematics and astrology into the country along with Catholic Christianity in the seventeenth century.

[16]Tai Il Wang, "Performing the Scripture: Understanding the Bible from Korean Biblical Hermeneutics," in *Mapping and Engaging the Bible in Asian Cultures: Congress of the Society of Asian Biblical Studies 2008 Seoul Conference*, ed. Yeong Mee Lee and Yoon Jong Yoo (Seoul: The Christian Literature Society of Korea, 2009), 47.

validations: (1) reading the Bible for herself releases the pathway to literacy that legitimizes her agency and dignity, and (2) reading the Bible as an imbiber, rather than as a biblical scholar, liberates her to relate to the God of the narratives in deeply connecting ways. Likening it to a musical piece in which each reader performs the text from their own station and culture, Wang suggests the biblical text, like the musical score, does not change, but the absorption of the text changes depending on the performer.[17]

Postcolonial interpretations. Out of these shifts and turns, postcolonial biblical hermeneutics emerged from the nations that had formerly been colonized under the European and later American colonial powers. Known as postcolonial theory, this body of literature focused on "the relationship between center and margin, metropolis and periphery, on a global political scale—the imperial and the colonial."[18] Even the recognition between these relationships in postcolonial theory shed light on the inherited biblical readings and interpretations from the center, the metropolis, and the imperial. Biblical hermeneutics conjoined to postcolonial theory means some of these interpretations from the colonial past need to be critically examined in order to seek a more liberative reading of the narratives found in Scripture.

Edward Said's postcolonial theory details the Orientalism versus Occidentalism binary. As a Palestinian-American, Said positions Orientalism as an expression used primarily by British and French colonists in confrontation with the Near Orient, Islam, and the Arab world. In particular, a strict boundary splits the two into binary spaces. Said writes, "The boundary notion of East and West, the varying degrees of projected inferiority and strength, the range of work done, the kinds of characteristic features ascribed to the Orient: all these testify to a willed imaginative and geographic division made between

---

[17]Wang, "Performing the Scripture," 50.
[18]Fernando F. Segovia, "Postcolonial and Diasporic Criticism in Biblical Studies: Focus, Parameters, Relevance," *Studies in World Christianity* 5 (1999): 180.

East and West, and lived through during many centuries."[19] This understanding of Orientalism has had a broad reach into theological spheres and has profoundly influenced Asian theologians.

Namsoon Kang, an Asian feminist theologian, extends the West's essentialization of the East in this way: "The typical image of the orient conceptualized by Orientalism is its strangeness, difference, exotic sensuousness, eccentricity, backwardness, silent indifference, feminine penetrability, uncivilized nature, and the like."[20] The manifestations of these essentializing acts take form in "homogenizing, tokenizing, ghettoizing, overgeneralization, oversimplification"[21] without accounting for the multifaceted and diverse social and cultural strata of class, gender, religion, ethnicity, and culture. This binary permits the Western colonizing of the East with dominance in all areas of life, including biblical interpretation and subsequent theological formations.

Postcolonial theory and theology identify this binary and seek liberation from these colonial structures. As such, many Asian and Asian American biblical scholars assert that a postcolonial interpretation of the Bible provides a multiplicity of contexts and perspectives where readers have agency to allow their social location to influence the process of interpretation rather than perpetuate a passive and docile reception of top-down, hegemonic interpretations from the West. In addition, within postcolonial readings of the Bible, could there be some understanding of the historical and cultural contexts of the text, utilizing parts of historical-cultural exegesis? Peter H. W. Lau contends, "Sensitivity to the world of the text needs

---

[19]Edward W. Said, *Orientalism* (New York: Pantheon Books, 1978), 201.
[20]Namsoon Kang, "Who/What Is Asian? A Postcolonial Theological Readings of Orientalism and Neo-Orientalism," in *Postcolonial Theologies: Divinity and Empire*, ed. Catherine Keller, Michael Nausner, and Mayra Rivera (St. Louis: Chalice Press, 2004), 102.
[21]Kang, "Who/What Is Asian?," 109. Kang identifies the other issue with Orientalism: the ahistoric sense of stagnancy that can be categorized and/or essentialized into an anonymous collectivity, like poverty, for instance. On the other hand, "Those frozen characteristics of the Orient sometimes are glorified, mystified, and idealized as the wisdom of the East, by both Western and Asian people," 103.

to become a more robust stream for postcolonial approaches to survive and leave a lasting mark."[22] In many ways, it coincides with Said's assertion that the "worldliness of text"—history, literature, politics, societal norms—impacts the reading and interpreting of the biblical text.[23]

Hebrew Bible scholar Gale Yee's definition of postcolonial interpretation and her understanding of its impact on Asian and Asian American identities is important here:

> Postcolonial interpretation takes seriously the biblical text, its reception history, and the global context of readers. This interpretation provides fertile ground for examining the overlapping concerns of hybridity, liminality, the third space, and the in-between space of the Asian and the Asian American identity and predicament.[24]

For example, Sugirtharajah provides what a postcolonial Asian reading of one of the most familiar parables might look like. Calling it "Chutnification," with new spice, color, and taste, he suggests reading the parable of the prodigal son (Luke 15) from the angle of the son who returns defeated to a father who shut him out by refusing "to grant his son's individuality and delights in his failure."[25] In this postcolonial reading, the classical perspective of the benevolent father is exchanged for the frustrated and oppressed son whose life reflects the patriarchal dominance of Asian parental control.

STOP AND THINK

- As you read the historical and contextual realities of Korea and how that context informs the reading of the Bible, what

---

[22]Peter Lau, "Another Postcolonial Reading of the Book of Ruth," in *Reading Ruth in Asia*, ed. Havea Jione and Peter H. W. Lau (Atlanta: SBL Press, 2015), 34.

[23]Edward W. Said, *The World, the Text, and the Critic* (Cambridge, MA: Harvard University Press, 1983), 39.

[24]Gale Yee, "Postcolonial Biblical Criticism," in *Methods for Exodus*, ed. T. B. Dozeman (New York: Cambridge University Press, 2010), 205-8. Cf. Sun, "Recent Research on Asian and Asian American Hermeneutics," 252.

[25]Sugirtharajah, *Asian Biblical Hermeneutics*, 96-97.

are the historical, cultural, and experiential contexts of your particular background that shape how you read the Bible?

- Similar to Orientalism, which typifies a massive group of people into a generalized stereotype, have you stereotyped or been stereotyped as inferior before? How might such stereotypes impede one's ability to exert freedom to fully represent oneself?

READING TEXTS

Through the varied lens of Asian biblical hermeneutics, we can read the familiar parable of the loving neighbor from the New Testament and the story of Ruth from the Hebrew Bible. These two well-known stories will highlight the difference in how intersectional readings can shed new light on familiar narratives.

The Parable of the Loving Neighbor (Luke 10:25-37)

The parable of the loving neighbor, more often referred to as the Good Samaritan, has been traditionally known to highlight the necessity of charitable, neighborly compassion. This is how the historical-critical interpretation of this pericope answers the questions the lawyer in the story asks: "What must I do to inherit eternal life?" (Luke 10:25) and "Who is my neighbor?" (Luke 10:29). Jesus elicits the *Shema*, "Hear O Israel," from Deuteronomy 6:4, when the lawyer answers, "You shall love the Lord your God with all your heart, and with all your soul, and with all your strength, and with all your mind; and your neighbor as yourself" (Luke 10:27). The Jewish hearers would immediately hearken to the daily prayer they recited morning and night, which is surrounded by the plea to be careful to obey the Ten Commandments in Deuteronomy 5 and Exodus 20. By prompting his hearers to recall the *Shema*, Jesus is setting up a subversive interpretation of this well-known and often-practiced prayer.

Jesus makes a Samaritan the hero of the parable he tells. Because of their differing religious beliefs and the locations of their sacred places of worship, the Samaritans were looked on as enemies by the Jews. In the minds of the hearers, a Samaritan may have been the very perpe- trator of robbing the man on his journey to Jerusalem rather than the savior. Here, one can just imagine the surprise when the parable of the loving neighbor elevates the despised Samaritans from the outer margins of the Jewish perspective to the center as a model of neigh- borly compassion. This differentiation between who is at the center and who is left at the margins shapes much of the Asian readings of this parable. In this short parable, Jesus exalts the despised Samaritan, the one who resides in the margins of suspicion, as the one who lives out the *Shema* of loving God and loving neighbor.

This subversive move of raising the least to the center is not lost on Asian biblical interpreters. Hunn Choi sees the Samaritan in this parable as the ultimate marginalized man whose peripheral identity becomes the very focus of God's vision. According to Choi, "He is a border crosser, a servant, and a new marginal man with a new center where his marginality does not diminish but exists on the center of the page of God's liberative story—no longer on the fringe, but at the center of a new story, a parable narrated by Jesus."[26] The important aspect of this interpretation is that the Samaritan retains all his identi- fiers of marginality, and these markers remarkably become the high- lighted center in Jesus' story. The last becomes the first.

Another Asian reading of this text is the missionary reading.[27] It also places the Samaritan at the center, but moreover, stations him as the significant figure of compassionate love. He is "a model of identi- fying with the oppressed; a model of transcending the traditional bar- riers of culture [race, ethnicity, class, religion, etc.] and creed while identifying with the needy; and a model of renouncing ritual purity

---

[26]Hunn Choi, "Multicultural Hermeneutics and Mission," *The Asbury Journal* 70, no.1 (2015), 127.
[27]While missionary readings have been critiqued elsewhere, not all missionary readings are problematic.

when ethical justice and mercy require it."[28] As a model who empathizes, crosses barriers, and works for justice, the oppressed Samaritan imitates an unmistakable representation of Jesus. Even in the Samaritan's humble, oppressed status, he exemplifies love and kindness.

The Indian Dalit (the "untouchables" of India's caste system) reading of this text takes this representation radically further by marking the Samaritan as the liberator. The Samaritan, the low-caste person who is stereotyped as one who remains at the margins of society, liberates the non-Dalit: "In this parable Jesus not only makes the Samaritan a liberating model for Jews to be a good neighbour to the oppressed, but he also means that Jews need Samaritans for their liberation."[29] In other words, the oppressors need the oppressed to emancipate them from blindness. Further, Indian theologian M. Gnanavaram clarifies this interpretation as God's characteristic preferential option for the oppressed:

> The biblical God is the God of the oppressed, and Jesus Christ is the supreme reference for God's preferential option for the poor and the oppressed through his life, death and resurrection: this option for the poor and the marginalized becomes the hermeneutical key in liberation hermeneutics. This option, in our context in India, concretely means option for the Dalits.[30]

The parable of the loving neighbor also extends to and undergirds the work of international development and community organizing with the poor from a Filipino woman's perspective. Jacqueline Aquino Siapno challenges the notion that the rich colonizers are the only ones who can show compassion. Siapno notices, "In international development work, there is barely any discussion of class (the fact that there are rich women and poor women, colonizing women and colonized

---

[28]M. Gnanavaram, "'Dalit Theology' and the Parable of the Good Samaritan," *JSNT* 50 (1993): 80-81.

[29]Gnanavaram, "Dalit Theology," 81. Jesus was equated to a Samaritan in John 8:48: "The Jews answered him, 'Aren't we right in saying that you are a Samaritan and have a demon?'"

[30]Gnanavaram, "Dalit Theology," 59.

women, urban women and rural women, old women and young women)."[31] The hierarchies are flattened. Like this parable, all people who are involved in global work are fellow travelers on the road, regardless of class. It may mean that a person from a despised people group is the one who rescues the colonizer.

Such reading is a part of larger readings of Scripture that offer deliverance to both the oppressor and oppressed through their mutuality of care. Chinese American theologian Kwok Pui-lan insists, "Postcolonial critics see biblical texts as more complex and multilayered and do not construct rich/poor, colonizer/colonized, and oppressor/oppressed in binary and dichotomous ways."[32] Similarly, Korean American theologian Heup Young Kim conveys this nuanced interrelated reading with Confucianism's relational model: "A reason why Confucianism is so attractive to the people in this postmodern period is because it does not conceive of a person as an isolated ego (individual) but as a center of relatedness in the network of communal relationships (relational/communal view)." From these Asian optics, one's salvation in separation with one's own community does not make sense.[33] Further, one is not the active giver and the other the passive recipient; rather, both are transformed. These selections of Asian readings of the parable reorient the savior to the margins and away from the traditional interpretations of the parable.

While these subversive readings of the parable are important, the interrogation of the very system that requires rescuers is also paramount. Japanese theologian Kosuke Koyama questions the multiple systems of

---

[31]Jacqueline Aquino Siapno, "Are There Good Samaritans? Beyond Local Gender Systems and Global Standards," *Asian Journal of Women's Studies* 16, no. 4 (2010), 93-94. Siapno's work on international relief efforts can be used to inform the lack of a dialogical relationship between the Samaritan and the wounded man. In relief work, like the wounded man, everyone's identity, name, and social location matters, and these identifiers may have a significant effect on the story through a mutual relational exchange.

[32]Kwok Pui-lan, "Reading the Christian New Testament in the Contemporary World," in *Fortress Commentary on the Bible: The New Testament*, ed. Margaret Aymer, Cynthia Briggs Kittredge, and David A. Sanchez (Minneapolis: Fortress, 2014), 20.

[33]Heup Young Kim, *Christ & the Tao* (Hong Kong: Christian Conference of Asia, 2003), 128.

injustice and power inequity that makes the Jericho road a dangerous place, replete with thievery and robbery. Koyama calls this very system into question. How can the system that makes spaces like the Jericho road be transformed? He proceeds, "For a long time it was fashionable in Asia to say that white domination had brutalized the Asians. Since 1950 this theme has rapidly become anachronistic. What we see today is that Asians are persecuting and murdering fellow Asians."[34] Koyama's call for systemic change may be grounded in imperial Japan's brutality and violence exerted over most of East and Southeast Asia during its imperial reign (1868–1945). He asserts, "In the human community the powerful are always beating up the weak. Victims are continually produced. . . . The Good Samaritan of today must be concerned with the change of the social systems. He must be interested in prevention of exploitation and victimization, and not just in taking care of victims left half-dead."[35] In other words, Koyama exhorts the hearers of this parable to be in the business of preventing victimization by working for systemic transformation of imbalanced power distribution.

Ruth the Migrant

The book of Ruth is a narrative of a Moabite woman who becomes a migrant by choice: a foreigner who disrupts the norms of a society that customarily shuns the stranger. In *Reading Ruth in Asia*, Jione Havea and Peter H. W. Lau note three broad Asian locations: people in Asia, people in the Asian diaspora (migration within Asia and around the globe), and people returning to their own Asian nation (re-migration).[36] Given these general classifications, Naomi can be seen as a migrant and a re-migrant while Ruth, a Moabite, is a migrant.

It may be assumed that Ruth's clothing, mannerisms, and her use of Hebrew language constantly divulged her Moabite origin;

---

[34]Kosuke Koyama, *Three Mile an Hour God*, 2nd ed. (London: SCM, 2021), 157.
[35]Koyama, *Three Mile an Hour God*, 157-58.
[36]Jione Havea and Peter H. W. Lau, "Reading Ruth Again, in Asia," in Havea and Lau, *Reading Ruth in Asia*, 4.

throughout the text she is consistently named "Ruth the Moabite" and sometimes even reflexively "Ruth the Moabite of Moab." The significance of her ethnic origin would not have been lost on the original readers and hearers of this story, since Moabite ancestry is traced to a son born from Lot and his eldest daughter after the destruction of Sodom (Genesis 19:37). Further, Moabite women have already appeared previously in Scripture as hypersexualized foreign women who brought idols and thereby punishment to Israel.[37] Hence, Moabites and Israelites were depicted as sworn enemies, except in a few instances, such as Deuteronomy 2 and 1 Samuel 22.

The conflicted relationship of Israelites and Moabites invites a subversive reading of this book. This is all the more significant if one considers that the book is named after a Moabite woman whose son is the grandfather of King David, an Israelite. Her identity as "Ruth the Moabite of Moab" can itself be the source of the subversive nature of this book, since Moabites were excluded from Israelite society. The theme of identity is woven throughout the Asian reading of Ruth, since an individual's identity is tightly embedded within a community in most Asian cultural contexts. Is Ruth betraying her own community? Is she a person without an identity because she has no ties to her original community? Is her hyphenated identity legitimate? Writing from a South Asian perspective, M. J. Melanchthon sees Ruth as an asylum seeker in a foreign land. This Asian feminist interpretation goes beyond Western feminist interpretations that remain mostly gender-focused; Asian feminist interpretations "see the interconnections that exist between women's oppression and cultural systems such as caste, religion, ethnicity and language."[38] In these

---

[37]Moabite women are the temptresses of Israelite men (Numbers 25:1-5); Moabites cannot be part of the Israelites (Deuteronomy 23:2-6); and Ezra and Nehemiah continue to exclude the Moabites in the postexilic period (Ezra 9:1–10:44; Nehemiah 13:1-3). See Wai-Ching Angela Wong, "History, Identity and a Community of *Hesed*: A Biblical Reflection on Ruth 1:1-17," *Asia Journal of Theology*, no. 13 (1999): 5-6.

[38]M. J. Melanchthon, "Toward Mapping Feminist Biblical Interpretations in Asia," in *Feminist Biblical Studies in the Twentieth Century: Scholarships and Movement*, ed. E. S. Fiorenza, Bible and Women 9.1 (Atlanta: SBL, 2014), 118.

intersections of various systems, Ruth has to at once recognize her identity simultaneously as a disadvantage and an advantage.

Katharine Sakenfeld's understanding of Ruth and Naomi's narrative, as couched in the tension between daily survival and concerns of kinship, is helpful for understanding intersectional identities.[39] She reads Ruth in the light of Southeast Asian women in red light districts. These women's entrapment into prostituted bodies clashes with their family values and the dire needs of their economic plight. Southeast Asian women find comfort in the story of Ruth and Naomi, wherein women must survive under parallel systems of gender, class, and ethnic oppression by recognizing all (dis)advantages of one's identities and leveraging them in relationship with others.

Similarly, Hong Kong–based culture and religion professor Wai-Ching Angela Wong writes, "Ruth is a story that addresses most tellingly the question of identity amidst ethnic rivalries and conflicts."[40] For Ching, the story of Ruth is a contestation of the notion that Israelite identity is only through genealogy. Through Ruth's compassionate (*hesed*) devotion to Naomi, and later to Boaz, Ruth's bearing of a son earns her a place in the Bethlehemite genealogy. *Hesed* is one of those words that defies easy translation. Hence we often get compound-word translations like "lovingkindness" or "steadfast love" or "covenant loyalty/faithfulness." A significant theme of this narrative, *hesed* can be defined in syntactical proximity to an Asian language. For example, Uriah Kim, a Korean Hebrew Bible scholar, explains the meaning of *hesed* in terms of the Korean word *jeong*.

> I use the Korean word *jeong* because I think it really captures the "affection-and-kindness" side of *hesed.* It is the loyalty side of *hesed* that maintains and strengthens existing relationships and the *jeong* side that

---

[39]Katharine Doob Sakenfeld, *Just Wives? Stories of Power and Survival in the Old Testament and Today* (Louisville, KY: Westminster John Knox Press, 2003), 27-48.

[40]Wai-Ching Angela Wong, "Identity in Hybridity: Ruth in the Genealogy of Jesus: Matthew 1:1-17; Ruth 1-4," *Theologies and Cultures* 6, no. 2 (2009): 99.

not only lubricates an existing relationship, but also allows new relations to be formed, even across various identity boundaries.[41]

Kim further posits that "Ruth refuses to go back to her mother's house and is resolved to become a migrant by accompanying her mother-in-law Naomi (Ruth 1:16-17) because there is a 'stickiness' (a main characteristic of *jeong*) in their relationship that cannot be easily severed."[42]

This loyal and kind side of *hesed* adds a strongly subversive nature to the text. It is a woman from the often hated and excluded Moabites that shows compassion to her Israelite mother-in-law. Wong argues, "One of the valuable lessons of the story of Naomi and Ruth is its ability to recognize the contribution of minorities to a dominant society and the willingness to reconcile rivalries between communities."[43] Put another way, the *hesed* represented in Ruth demonstrates that as an ethnic minority, Ruth is able to create new possibilities of life not only for herself but also others in that traditional dominant culture. Ruth offers this *hesed* toward Boaz by accepting him as her relative. He redeems her father-in-law's field, and together they perpetuate the family line by producing a son (Ruth 3:12-13).[44]

Conversely, many Asian American biblical scholars who struggle against the myth of the model minority in the Asian diasporic communities of North America resonate with Laura Donaldson, a Native American scholar who argues that the book of Ruth is the Israelite version of the "Pocahontas Perplex." According to Donaldson, this perplex is a strategy White people constructed to advance Native American women who aided and even saved White people as noble

---

[41]Uriah Y. Kim, "Where Is the Home for the Man of Luz?," *Interpretation* 65, no. 3 (2011): 256.

[42]Kim, "Where Is the Home for the Man of Luz?," 250-62. See also Ching, "History, Identity and a Community of *Hesed*"; Angela Son, "*Jeong* as the Paradigmatic Embodiment of Compassion (*Hesed*): A Critical Examination of Disparate and Dispositional *Jeong*," *Pastoral Psychology* 63, nos. 5-6 (Dec 2014): 735-47.

[43]Wong, "Identity in Hybridity," 109.

[44]See Lau, "Another Postcolonial Reading of the Book of Ruth," 23.

princesses—a sort of model minority.[45] As such, the narrative of Ruth resonates with Asian Americans who are known as the perpetual foreigners due to their phenotype (physical, observable characteristics of genetic and environmental influences).

While Asian Americans are unable to shake off the stranger stigma, it is juxtaposed with the model minority myth. The narrative read from a Moabite perspective resembles this tension. Ruth is constantly reminded of her foreigner identity and yet performs as a model minority, exemplifying pure loyalty. She remains a perpetual foreigner even to the point of becoming a hidden figure whose name is dropped from the narrative after she births a son in Ruth 4:13.[46] It is Naomi the Israelite who takes the son "and laid him in her bosom, and became his nurse" (Ruth 4:16). She is admired by the village women, who name the child Obed.

Ruth's invisibility after being held up as a model minority is what Yee attributes to the "racial melancholia" that is clearly displayed in the book of Ruth. Yee describes racial melancholia as "the psychic condition of unarticulated loss, experienced by racialized groups living in a dominant culture."[47] She ties this condition of "unarticulated grief" of Ruth to diasporic Asians in America, in particular, who are never fully embraced as Americans despite their manifold negotiation efforts to assimilate.

Postcolonial reading interrogates the method of Ruth's subversive identity and gives clarity to what Yee may mean by "assimilate." In her hybrid identity as a Moabitess living in Israel, Ruth quickly

---

[45]For example, Uriah Kim and Kwok Pui-lan both prefer the Moabite perspective rather than the Jewish reception of Ruth, who then disappears in the narrative after the birth of Obed, who then is attributed to Naomi (Ruth 4:16-17). See Laura E. Donaldson, "The Sign of Orpah: Reading Ruth Through Native Eyes," in *The Postcolonial Biblical Reader*, ed. R. S. Sugirtharajah (Oxford: Blackwell, 2006).

[46]Gale Yee, "'She Stood in Tears amid the Alien Corn': Ruth, the Perpetual Foreigner and Model Minority," in *Off the Menu: Asian and Asian North American Women's Religion and Theology*, ed. Rita Nakashima Brock et al. (Louisville, KY: Westminster John Knox Press, 2007). Ruth is mentioned in Ruth 4:15 only as "your daughter-in-law . . . who is more to you than seven sons."

[47]Gale Yee, "Racial Melancholia in the Book of Ruth," in *The Five Scrolls*, ed. Gale A. Yee and Archie C. C. Lee (London: T&T Clark, 2018), 68.

acculturates to her new surroundings by imitating the ones at the center of Israelite society through what postcolonial theorist Homi Bhabha calls "mimicry."[48] Bhabha notes that mimicry resists the gaze of the colonizer or the dominant culture by gazing back. Such imitation, at the risk of being seen as assimilation, is a "form of mockery."[49] In this postcolonial understanding of imitation, "assimilation" may subvert the center since the imitation cannot be an exact replica but is by default done with a particular and perhaps intentional difference. As such, by "assimilation" through imitation or mimicry, Ruth gazes back at the dominant culture with her own sense of self rather than as a performative function of a model minority or perpetual foreigner.

REFLECTING ON THE TEXTS

- When you read the parable of the loving neighbor, what aspects are highlighted if you remember that the neighbor is a Samaritan? How does reading a biblical story from the margins differ from reading it from the center?

- What are one or two "Jericho roads" or systems of injustice and power inequity in your contexts? What are one or two ways you can disrupt that system toward transformation?

- How do the intersections of class, gender, sexuality, race, ethnicity, and language in reading Ruth broaden the meaning of biblical stories to emphasize the liberative move from such forms of oppression in God's overarching story?

---

[48]Sin-Lung Tong, "The Key to Successful Migration? Rereading Ruth's Confession (1:16-17) Through the Lens of Bhabha's Mimicry," in Jione and Lau, *Reading Ruth in Asia*, 35.
[49]David Huddart, *Homi Bhabha* (London: Routledge, 2006), 29; Homi Bhabha, *Location of Culture*, 2nd ed. (London: Routledge, 2004), 122-23; Tong, "The Key to Successful Migration?," 39.

CONCLUDING THOUGHTS

As we have seen, reading the Bible from many places dethrones the temptation to claim narrowly construed truth and to hold one inter- pretive lens as normative. Just as Asia is a nonhomogenous, non- monolithic entity, Asian interpretations reflect the multiple ways of reading scriptural texts that cannot be narrowed down to one Asian interpretation. As presented in this chapter, the three Western mo- dalities of reading the Bible (Orientalist, Anglicist, and Nativist) in some regions, such as India, have spread throughout various Asian countries through colonialism. For instance, the perspective from which the Bible was read in most of Asia came initially from Euro- Americans who distilled it from their context and disseminated this perspective to various mission areas. Biblical scholar Elisabeth Shüssler Fiorenza clarifies this implicit tendency:

> Because of the all-too-human need to use the Bible to bolster our identity over and against that of others, because of the need for using the Bible as a security blanket—as an avenue for controlling the divine, or as a means for possessing revelatory knowledge as an exclusive privilege— biblical interpreters are ever tempted to build up securing walls and to keep out those who are not like us.[50]

Furthering or jettisoning those modalities, different Asian bib- lical scholars have interpreted Scripture based on their various con- texts and particularities. From various cultural, social, and geographical places in the larger contexts of Asia, the nuance offered through these works provides holistic possibilities. That is, the whole picture of the reading of the Bible may only be possible if manifold interpretations from various social locations are gathered together in a kaleidoscope of readings. As such, the varied Asian contextual approaches to reading Scripture suggest the unseating of Western centrism, the end of the universalization of Western

---

[50]Elisabeth Schüssler Fiorenza, *Democratizing Biblical Studies: Toward an Emancipatory Educa- tional Space* (Louisville, KY: Westminster John Knox, 2009), 150.

theology, and the inclusion of various perspectives and voices of previously marginalized groups.

Asian readings of the biblical texts offer such surprises and transformational possibilities. Being free from "colonial" readings of Scripture posits the possibility of the intent and purpose of the biblical texts. Each group, and individual within the group, can gain fresh relationship with the God of the Bible by reading the biblical texts through one's specific context, experiences, and intersectional identities. Notably, the multivalent readings of the parable of the loving neighbor from the Dalit perspective posit the Dalit as the liberator who emancipates the oppressor. Such readings establish the mutual interdependence of the oppressed and the oppressor and shed light on how one must work toward systemic changes that promote justice and equity. Additionally, the Asian readings of Ruth's migrant status provide stronger metaphors for the leveraging of one's (dis)advantaged identities. More specifically, assimilation may be a form of mimicry that interrogates the system and demands the proper treatment of its racial melancholia. Inherent in these readings is the possibility that we may be surprised and even be transformed by these multiperspectival readings of even familiar biblical texts.

CONSIDERING THE WHOLE

- Given that Asia is a vast geographic mass with multiple historical, religious, linguistic, and cultural differences, do you think it is possible to have one Asian biblical interpretation?

- How might a particular country's history of colonization influence the reading of the Bible? For instance, countries like China and Japan have never been under colonial rule, as opposed to other Asian nations that have.

SUGGESTIONS FOR FURTHER READING

Boer, Roland, and Fernando F. Segovia. *The Future of the Biblical Past: Envisioning Biblical Studies on a Global Key.* Society of Biblical Literature Semeia Studies. Atlanta: Society of Biblical Literature, 2012.

Cheng, Patrick S. "Multiplicity and Judges 19: Constructing a Queer Asian Pacific American Biblical Hermeneutic." *Semeia* 90–91 (2002): 119-33.

Choi, Hee An. *Korean Women and God: Experiencing God in a Multi-religious Colonial Context.* Maryknoll, NY: Orbis, 2005.

Kwok Pui-lan. *Postcolonial Imagination and Feminist Theology.* Louisville, KY: Westminster John Knox, 2005.

Lee, Jung Young. *Marginality: The Key to Multicultural Theology.* Minneapolis: Fortress, 1995.

Liew, Tat-Siong Benny. *What Is Asian American Biblical Hermeneutics? Reading the New Testament.* Intersections: Asian and Pacific American Transcultural Studies. Honolulu: University of Hawai'i Press, 2008.

Moore, Stephen D., and Fernando F. Segovia. *Postcolonial Biblical Criticism: Interdisciplinary Intersections.* The Bible and Postcolonialism. New York: T&T Clark, 2005.

Schüssler Fiorenza, Elisabeth. *Democratizing Biblical Studies: Toward an Emancipatory Educational Space.* Louisville, KY: Westminster John Knox, 2009.

Segovia, Fernando F. *Decolonizing Biblical Studies: A View from the Margins.* Maryknoll, NY: Orbis, 2000.

Sugirtharajah, R. S. *Asian Biblical Hermeneutics and Postcolonialism: Contesting the Interpretations.* Bible & Liberation Series. Maryknoll, NY: Orbis, 1998.

———. *Still at the Margins: Biblical Scholarship Fifteen Years After Voices from the Margin.* New York: T&T Clark, 2008.

Tan, Jonathan Y. *Introducing Asian American Theologies.* Maryknoll, NY: Orbis, 2008.

Yee, Gale, ed. *The Hebrew Bible: Feminist and Intersectional Perspectives.* Minneapolis: Fortress, 2018.

6

DIASPORIC APPROACHES

KAY HIGUERA SMITH

DIASPORA IS A TRANSLITERATED GREEK WORD that literally means "dispersion." In biblical tradition, it has been used to signify the dispersion of the people of Israel outside of their land. It is a central theme in the Bible, as the ancient Israelites needed to make sense of their experiences of dislocation and exile. In the contemporary world, we often hear of the African diaspora. This term refers to all those whose roots are in Africa but who are dispersed throughout the world, especially those whose ancestors were kidnapped and brought as slaves to North, South, and Central America and the Caribbean. Many people today experience less traumatic diaspora, whether it is by participating in our globalized economy, migrating from one country to another, or crossing borders because of economic or political hardship. Rarely do we hear sermons about the experience of diaspora. Yet this central biblical theme is very important for many Christians today. We will see that diaspora is a crucial category for understanding how people today interpret the Bible.

Diaspora names more than physical or geographic displacement. It also can name cultural or political displacement. Sometimes, a people can stay in one place for centuries while the larger culture changes over their lifetimes, causing them to experience diaspora while never leaving home. Consider, in this regard, indigenous people and Mexicans in California, Arizona, or New Mexico. Indigenous populations lived in these regions for tens of thousands of years before colonial expansion almost caused their extinction. Many indigenous communities survive on reservations, in remote regions, in ghettoes, or by keeping their memories alive through family and clan connections.

The first such diaspora occurred when Spain conquered these regions in the sixteenth century, resulting in genocide, conversion to a new religion—both forced and voluntary—and displacement for large populations. The second occurred in the late nineteenth century. At that time, thousands of Anglo-Europeans flowed into these regions because of the Gold Rush and took lands by squatting and by violence against the local populace. This led to the United States seizing the lands by force in the Mexican-American War (1846–1848), which resulted in our current borders. As a consequence, even more indigenous groups, now joined by Mexican settlers, lost their homes and their lives. In these ways, indigenous families on both sides of the border, some of whom were fully indigenous, some of whom were descended from those who had settled the region since the sixteenth century, were forced, over time, to experience or have a social memory of two major diasporas without ever leaving home.

Thus diaspora can be cultural, religious, or political. It takes on many forms and cannot be limited merely to geographic displacement. When I refer to the term in this chapter, I will consider both geographic and social/cultural diasporas as well as their effects. In all of these cases, however, I will consider those migrants and exiles who have their bodies acted on by external, coercive forces in the process of carrying out an offensive action through colonial expansion or unprovoked warfare.

Given that diasporas generally emerge out of coercive forces acting on a population, it should not surprise us that the experience of diaspora shapes how such populations create meaning. Social groups shape meaning out of their group expectations, values, cherished assumptions, and interests. Thus when a group experiences any social change, including diaspora, all of those elements will likely shift. This will result in a need to make meaning of the changes. Perhaps you have experienced this difference in meaning when sharing your scriptural understanding with a person from a group that does not share your assumptions. You may have found that the person with whom you are reading Scripture finds very different meaning in it than you do. Diaspora, power differentials, and cultural norms create new meanings, as well as new readings of biblical texts, by creating new ways of understanding the world and even understanding ourselves.

Diasporic identity often means not fitting into the norms of one's adopted culture. It would not be far-fetched to claim that every one of us is familiar with the experience of some kind of diasporic identity. Culturally, you may have grown up with one religion and converted to or adopted another. Politically, you may have received one set of values from your parents but may have grown to reject those in favor of a different value system. But in the above cases, this diasporic identity did not necessarily place you in a position of marginality vis-à-vis your former identity. On the other hand, there are many people for whom diasporic identity is associated with living on the cultural margins, or periphery.

Ethnically, those who are on the social/cultural periphery are very familiar with the notion of diasporic identity. For instance, W. E. B. Du Bois wrote about the "double consciousness" that African Americans experience in the United States. They develop one consciousness of who they are based on family and culture, but they also are forced by the dominant culture to recognize a second consciousness of who they are based on how the dominant culture perceives them.[1] That second consciousness—that of being aware of how the dominant culture perceives you—also shapes identity, whether or not that transformed identity is welcomed by the individual. This is a kind of diasporic identity borne out of the experience of being on the periphery of cultural power.

The power to define what is normative is a power uniquely held by the dominant, nondiasporic culture in any situation. In exercising this power to define what is normative, the dominant culture automatically names as deviant those who are not part of its culture. Because of this, diasporic identities that are on the social periphery manifest the greatest amount of social/cultural anxiety, but they also tend to be the most innovative in their interpretations of socially important texts like the Bible. The "double consciousness" of navigating the dominant culture's expectations as well as one's own is the challenge to which we now turn.

IDENTITY AS HYBRIDITY

Members of diasporic groups and communities must make their way in a world that names them as deviant. They must master the idioms and norms of the dominant culture from their own social space, which has bequeathed to them very different norms and idioms. This hyphenated, diasporic identity results in a kind of hybrid, intersectional way of viewing one's own group. That is, exiles, immigrants, migrants, and sojourners develop both group and individual identities that are shaped by these various social, cultural, gendered, ethnic, racial, physiological, economic, geographic, and historical forces. These forces often elicit in diasporic folks anxiety, fear, or silencing, but also adaptation, innovation, and resistance. All of these reactions matter when people in diasporic communities read their sacred Scriptures.

---

[1]W. E. B. Du Bois, *The Souls of Black Folk* (Rockville, MD: Arc Manor, 2007), 12.

Often these various forces make competing claims on group members. For instance, I myself benefit, as a bicultural woman—half Anglo-European and half Mexican—from my ability to operate freely in the dominant culture. But I also challenge the dominant culture because of the questions with which my Latina identity affords me. I am both colonizer and colonized, and I move efficiently and almost unconsciously in and out of both spheres. My intersectional identity challenges the cherished myths of the dominant culture but also benefits from those myths. Hybrid identity is not neat and fixed. It is fluid and shifting.

Jamal is a young African American man who grew up in the very conservative suburbs of Orange County, California. On one hand, because of his race, Jamal has experienced unwarranted harassment by police and overwrought suspicion by some neighbors. On more than one occasion, police have stopped him for small, invented traffic violations. Sometimes the police have tried to goad him with false accusations in an effort to get him to become defensive—apparently, he has concluded, so that they can escalate the traffic stop into something more serious. He has had to learn to address their concerns calmly and to ignore the harassment. In this sense, the message that the culture sends him is that he is marginal and threatening. On the other hand, because of the friendships he has forged with more welcoming Anglo-European neighbors, he does not ascribe to all White people the charge of racial harassment. His hybrid identity—African American living in an affluent White suburban community—causes him to see things differently than someone might who is living in an exclusively African American community undergoing similar treatment by police officers. He has become an accomplished artist, and his art, which challenges the status quo, is well received in his community. Nevertheless, he is deeply aware of his own marginalization and tenuous existence because of the fixed norms of the larger White community. He has learned to adapt and negotiate those competing claims along with their carefully policed boundaries. His hybridized identity allows him to parlay his hyphenated identity in innovative ways while resisting and challenging the racialized norms of his community.

These competing claims of hybrid identity show up in other ways as well. Homi Bhabha describes how the notion of disrespect in South Central Los Angeles is a form of hybridity. In that inner city context, young people often experience the "double consciousness" of seeing themselves through the lens of the more powerful dominant culture, a culture that neither respects nor trusts them. In reaction to this consciousness, demanding respect becomes a primary goal. Because of this, members of one inner city group—be they Black, Latino/a, Asian, or White—may incite violence against members of another even though both groups share a history of being discriminated against and being disrespected by the dominant culture, and even though both groups share other diasporic experiences and identities, they may commit violence against each other partly in response to the disrespect that they experience from the dominant culture. They hurt both their own self-interest and that of their victims.[2]

Dorothea and J.R. also live in South Central Los Angeles. Dorothea is a school administrator and J.R. is a retired teacher. They have been married for many years and have successfully raised a beautiful family. They have spent a lifetime negotiating hybridized identities, often by code-switching and fending off microaggressions. While they've done so successfully, it nevertheless has taken its toll. Both Dorothea and J.R. speak of exhaustion in having to negotiate daily interactions that sap their energy. The power of the dominant culture to set the norms puts in motion social forces that coerce individuals to find ways to manage the diasporic experience.

The above examples show that hybridity is rarely neat and clean. It always responds to the physical or social violence of the dominant culture and seeks to make sense of social forces that name it as

---

[2]Homi Bhabha, *The Location of Culture*, 2nd ed. (New York: Routledge, 2006), 3.

deviant. These forces can cause diasporic groups to break out against the hybrid within themselves as well as against those who share diasporic identities with them, as in the case of urban youths. But they also can result in people creating new, fluid identities that allow for interactions and creative new meanings, new creations, and new art that are rich and life giving, as in the cases of Jamal, Dorothea, and J.R., all of whom both adapted and resisted. These new meanings often translate into new interpretations of the Bible as well.

RESTAGING THE PAST

One way that diasporic communities deal with hybrid, or retraditionalized, identities, argues Bhabha, is to "restage the past"—to revisit history and view it anew from the perspective of those who in the past did not have the social/cultural power to write that history.[3] We see this in the efforts by indigenous people in the Americas to highlight the injustices done to them by the US government. We see it in efforts by marginalized groups to highlight forgotten artists, writers, inventors, and innovators—key figures whose contributions to culture have either been forgotten or downplayed by those who had the social power to write the histories and define the norms. One example of this is that many people today have a newfound interest in the scriptural importance of Africa and in African interpretations of Scripture. They seek to reimagine ways of reading and finding meaning in the Bible that resisted the readings of the colonial era, which sought to erase the significance of Africans in the Bible.[4] Another example is the effort by Japanese Americans to revisit the forced incarceration of Japanese in internment camps during World War II.[5] As marginalized groups gain social power through education or social/cultural change,

[3]Bhabha, *Location of Culture*, 4.
[4]See Hugh R. Page et al., eds., *The Africana Bible: Reading Israel's Scriptures from Africa and the African Diaspora* (Minneapolis: Fortress, 2009).
[5]Mary Matsuda Gruenewald, *Looking Like the Enemy: My Story of Imprisonment in Japanese American Internment Camps* (Troutdale, OR: NewSage Press, 2005).

opportunities open up for them to have a voice in their cultural worlds. A key strategy for identity formation in these cases is to "re-stage" and reconstruct the past by rejecting the readings of their own group's history that the dominant culture puts forward.

But it isn't just those on the periphery who restage the past. Dominant cultures do it all the time because they have the resources to do so. Roni Dean-Burren received a text from her fifteen-year-old son, Coby, containing a picture of a map of the United States taken from Coby's high school textbook, which was published in Texas. In a small text box pointing to the Southern US states, it stated that the Atlantic slave trade brought workers from Africa to the southern United States to work on agricultural plantations.[6] For Roni and her son, who are African American, this attempt to rename African slaves as "workers" was one more way for the dominant culture to control the way that knowledge is produced so that it suppresses and cloaks the very well-remembered terror that the slave trade brings to mind among those in the African diaspora who live in the United States. Schoolbook selection is overseen by school boards that are often dominated by those who do not know their own history and do not want the next generation to know the depth of cruelty and terror that marked that era. By controlling how and what knowledge is produced, the guardians of the dominant culture create social memories that "re-stage" the past. But their restaging is for the purpose of silencing and minimizing those narratives that make them uncomfortable. While one member of the Texas Board of Education insisted that this was an isolated case and that elsewhere the book did treat slavery accurately, nevertheless the case brought to the public's attention the highly political nature of textbook writing and editing. It demonstrates how "restaging the past" has always gone on, but it generally has been in

---

[6]Laura Isensee, "How Texas Board, Publisher Hope to Prevent Mistakes After Mom Calls out Reference to Slaves in Textbook," October 13, 2015, www.houstonpublicmedia.org/articles/news/2015/10/13/124382/how-texas-board-publisher-hope-to-prevent-mistakes-after-mom-calls-out-reference-to-slaves-in-textbook.

the context of the dominant culture seeking to control how knowledge is produced, making the need for "restaging" even more urgent for diasporic groups.[7]

These examples show us how identity is closely connected with meaning. How communities understand and formulate their histories has a direct correlation with their own critical questions. Social memory includes social forgetting, which can be effective for dominant cultures. However, it cloaks and obscures important historical events that may challenge the values of that culture. In this way, meaning and identity are intertwined.

DIASPORIC ENCOUNTERS WITH THE LOVING NEIGHBOR (LUKE 10:25-35)

Hybrid, or diasporic, identity thus can result in approaches to meanings that display this complexity. These meanings are not purely good or purely evil. They are complex. Whether those meanings involve a restaging of the past, a refusal to participate in the social "forgetting" of the dominant culture, a resignifying of symbols or codes, or even a recapitulating of the violence that diasporic communities experience in order to gain what looks to them like "respect"—all of these are efforts to create new meaning in the face of hybridized or hyphenated social realities. These new approaches challenge the powerful social constructions of the dominant culture, on one hand, while on the other they employ the dominant culture's own idioms and stated values to do so. New meanings emerge as new, diasporic identities are formed.

These meanings apply to the interpretation of Scripture as well. As we have learned in previous chapters, biblical Israelites lived in diaspora for most of their histories—either real diasporas or those

---

[7]Laura Isensee, "Why Calling Slaves 'Workers' Is More Than an Editing Error," October 23, 2015, www.npr.org/sections/ed/2015/10/23/450826208/why-calling-slaves-workers-is-more -than-an-editing-error.

created as products of social memories. The heirs of the ancient Israelites, the Jews, still recite today at Passover YHWH's famous command to Moses to proclaim that "a wandering Aramean was my ancestor; he went down into Egypt and lived there as an alien, few in number, and there he became a great nation, mighty and populous" (Deuteronomy 26:5). By reciting these words, Jews even to this day remind themselves through their liturgy to see themselves as wanderers, migrants, and strangers. They recite and practice diasporic, hybrid identity, thus giving it a hallowed position in Jewish meaning-making.

Bhabha's discussion of hybridity allows us to understand and make sense of diasporic readings. When a social group undergoes a massive social transformation, such as what occurs during a major drought, famine, forced migration, forced exile, or genocide, the group's members interpret their Scripture, their history, and their current events in light of that cataclysmic event.

A good example—to build on the work of preceding chapters—is the case of the Samaritans. Christians in the United States today tend to understand the word *Samaritan* as a product of our own social needs and critical questions. But the meaning they ascribe to it is not necessarily the same as the meaning that the ancient hearers of the gospel would have ascribed to it or what Israelis, including modern Samaritans in Israel, would ascribe to it today.

The word *Samaritan* comes from the region in central Israel called Samaria, or, in Hebrew, *Shomron*. The city of Samaria/*Shomron* was the capital of the northern kingdom of Israel when the northern and southern kingdoms split during the reign of Solomon's son Rehoboam in the tenth century BCE. Later, in 722 BCE, the Assyrian Empire conquered the northern kingdom and exiled the local populace (2 Kings 17:6; see also 2 Kings 18:11-12). Those remaining in the land were called Samarians, and later, Samaritans. The narrator of 2 Kings 17:24-41 stated that Assyria repopulated Samaria with refugees from other regions it had conquered and that those refugees brought in religious practices from their homelands. In this way, the narrator provided a justification for the wide gulf that had grown between Samaria and the heirs of the southern kingdom by the time of the writing of 2 Kings. The heirs of the southern kingdom, on the other hand, were called Judahites (Hebrew: *yehudim*), a name derived from the tribe of Judah, which was dominant in that region. The Hebrew word *yehudim* is translated as "Jews" in English. Hence the Jews were those who descended from the southern kingdom and whose priests, prophets, and sages passed down to us the Hebrew Bible as we know it. As we have seen, these kinds of calamitous changes result in very real social/cultural changes, which in turn result in changes in meaning. By the first century CE, relations between the Samaritans and the Jews were hostile. The Jewish high priest John Hyrcanus had destroyed the Samaritan temple on Mount Gerizim in 110 BCE, making the hostilities even more severe. Both groups—Samaritans and Jews—possessed their own versions of the Torah, and neither group would accept the other.

This is the ancient context for the story of the loving neighbor in Luke 10:25-35. In Luke, when Jesus told the story, the Samaritan would have been considered a schismatic and an apostate, or heretic, by the Jewish people. It is in this context that Jesus' description of the Samaritan is so significant. Jesus describes him as acting more consistently with the divine law of love than did the two figures in the story who had high religious standing among Jesus' people. Put another way, Jesus challenged his audience by claiming that the Samaritan— the perceived "apostate" in their world—was more faithful to God's divine law of love than were those whom the people looked up to as having correct doctrine and religious standing. In the first-century context, this story was a challenge by Jesus to those in his dominant culture to cross boundaries and learn from those whom they had marked as deviant or dangerous.

That is not the meaning, however, that many US Christians ascribe to this story. In my university classes, when I ask my students what they know about Samaritans, the typical answer is that they are good! After all, this is the story of the "Good Samaritan"! In fact, a short internet search brings up the names of several nonprofit organizations with "Samaritan" in the name, denoting those who engage in charitable or humanitarian work. In today's lexicon, at least in the United States, no longer does Samaritan mean an Israelite non-Jew or even a schismatic from a Jewish perspective. This is the case despite the fact that Samaritan communities still thrive in Israel. Instead, in the US context, it refers to a humanitarian or a self-sacrificing giver. The challenge to religious and cultural status and the diasporic nature of the story has been erased. No more is the Samaritan a challenge to the status quo. Now he is just a "good" guy whom we all should emulate by being "good" ourselves. The story has been stripped of its subversive meaning that challenges the religious status quo.

The Gospel of Luke is the only Gospel to tell us this story of the "Good Samaritan." It is striking that it is in this Gospel where we find this diasporic reading that radically challenges social conventions. Luke's Gospel, more than any other, focuses on the poor. In Luke's version of the beatitude, he has Jesus saying, "Blessed are you who are poor" (Luke 6:20). There is no mention of the "poor in spirit" that Matthew's Jesus blesses (cf. Matthew 5:30). Luke's Jesus simply blesses the poor, showing that our Gospel writer aligned himself with those who had no money and were oppressed. The parable of the Samaritan in Luke fits Luke's community, who make meaning out of their hybridized, marginalized, social/cultural experience. Interpretations in powerful communities, however, which have an interest in preserving the status quo, suppress the subversive meaning of the story and turn the Samaritan into a benign, nonthreatening character.

The above example should not cause us to assume, however, that our New Testament authors never developed social identities that "wrote out" those who were social/cultural others. Paul, despite being Jewish himself, often used language that seems to construct Jewish people (who had not accepted Jesus as the Messiah for the Jews) as the binary other whom he wants his hearers to resist and vanquish. To be sure, even today, scholars of Paul's epistles dispute whether he intentionally or unintentionally meant his words to be used to attack Jews. Nevertheless, whatever Paul's intent, later generations of Christian leaders consistently assigned a hostile meaning to Paul's writings about the Jews in order to justify their persecution and church-sponsored terror against Jews. A good example is in Galatians 4:30. Citing Genesis 21:10, Paul writes, "Drive out the slave and her child; for the child of the slave will not share the inheritance with the child of the free woman." Paul here calls for his hearers to "drive out" those with whom he disagrees. Is Paul here referring to the Jewish people, or is he referring merely to those Jesus followers who seek to limit access to the people of God? The meaning that the reader derives will most likely correspond to the interests of the group to which the reader belongs. In either case, however, Paul's words are not those of hospitality but of setting up clear, binary distinctives in social identity and hence in meaning. Those words can and have been used to support violence against the Jewish people as well as other groups in history that threaten dominant cultural identities.

People are making meaning all over the world in our pulpits, our prayer groups, and our Bible studies. However, if we are not aware of how meaning shifts, we might mistakenly import meanings into the Bible or uncritically apply to ourselves meanings in the Bible that reflect our own needs to create "us and them" identities. Those who live with the complexities and intersectionalities of this world will take seriously whose meanings they are "writing out" of Scripture and whose meanings they are "enshrining" in Scripture. If people enshrine only those meanings that reinforce the perspective of the powerful, then they may be missing other, equally valid, and perhaps even prophetic voices of Scripture for their communities. We should not fear or be discomforted by these shifts in meaning-making. Those who are exiles, migrants, or persecuted must find new meanings in order to move ahead. If they do not, the Bible will cease to be meaningful at all.

DISCOVERING AND LIVING OUT NEW MEANINGS

Elie Wiesel was a young boy when he was sucked into the jaws of the *Shoah*—or Holocaust, as it is better known. Wiesel was born in Romania in 1928 to Jewish parents. During World War II, he was thrown into the Auschwitz Concentration Camp at age fifteen, a camp in which the Nazis killed over a million Jewish people. In the camp, he was forced at a very young age to make sense of the cataclysm that shattered his world. Somehow, he survived. Years later, Wiesel reflected on how that experience shaped his reading of the Bible. He had been raised to accept Deuteronomy's response to catastrophe, which asserts that ancient Israel called its fate on itself because of its sins. This answer, which satisfied some of the biblical authors in a very different social-historical context, could not stand or make any sense to him in the face of the horrors of the Holocaust. He indeed was witnessing sin, but it was not his people's sin that he was witnessing. Wiesel explained that as a child he had been taught that "it is because of our sins that we had been exiled." But in Auschwitz he rejected that interpretation, asserting, "No, it is not because of our sins. There were no sins, not that many. I refuse to believe that there could have been so many sins to provoke such a punishment. If there was such a punishment, it is because someone else had sinned, not we, not the people of Israel."[8]

Wiesel demonstrated this conviction in a scene in his novel *Night*, which is set in Auschwitz. In the novel, a horrifying event takes place.

---

[8]Elie Wiesel, "My Teachers," radio address, Eternal Light Series, Jewish Theological Seminary, New York. Cited in Michael Berenbaum, *Elie Wiesel: God, the Holocaust, and the Children of Israel* (West Orange, NJ: Behrman House, 1994), 13.

The Nazi concentration camp overseers hang two men and a small boy for minor infractions. But the small boy does not die right away. Instead, he suffers a slow, agonizing death. What is this little boy's sin that he should suffer so? The classic answer from Deuteronomy is that there must be sin in the boy's life that has led him to this point. That answer crumbles in the face of Auschwitz. Wiesel describes the scene:

> For more than half an hour he [the boy] stayed there, struggling between life and death, dying in slow agony under our eyes. . . . He was still alive when I passed in front of him. His tongue was still red, his eyes were not yet glazed. Behind me, I heard the same man asking, "Where is God now?" And I heard a voice within me answer him: "Where is He? Here he is—He is hanging here on this gallows."[9]

Like the followers of Jesus, who had to make sense of goodness hanging on a gallows, Wiesel could not find God in the classic answers of his tradition. The *caesura*—the absolute rupture—that was Auschwitz, characterized by cruel meaninglessness and horrific death, changed the meaning of God's own nature for Wiesel forever. In moments of historic disruption such as Wiesel and millions of others experience, new meanings must emerge, because the old meanings collapse under the weight of catastrophe.

It is in this way that the Bible makes new sense of people's experiences, especially in the light of migration, border crossing, and exile. These experiences cause people to ask new questions and find new meanings. Phillip Connor, in his 2014 book *Immigrant Faith: Patterns of Immigrant Religion in the United States, Canada, and Western Europe,* tells of a recent Chinese immigrant to Canada named Guo Kai Li. Guo Kai Li was raised, like so many others in mainland China, by parents who had rejected religion and any notion of a god. Yet, after immigrating to Montreal and experiencing the upheaval, disorientation, and disruption that are common among immigrants,

---

[9]Elie Wiesel, *Night; Dawn; The Accident: A Trilogy* (New York: Hill and Wang, 2004), 75.

she began to recall the Bible stories that her grandmother had told her back in China. On meeting some other Chinese immigrants who were Christians, she began to attend their Bible study group. Connor writes, "She found that the church meetings gave her a peace she had not sensed before, especially given the turmoil of adjusting to a new place."[10] Chinese immigrants in the United States and Canada often report strong experiences of marginalization. Some of that is due to their unfamiliarity with the strong Christian presence in the United States and Canada, and some is due to social and cultural differences. Guo Kai Li found in the Chinese Christian Bible study group a way to deal with these experiences. Soon she requested to be baptized as a Christian. Her immigrant experience brought her face to face with questions that she had ignored or failed to consider in her previous life in China. The Bible stories that she had heard as a child began to take on new meanings in her new context. Connor is quick to point out that immigration does not generally lead to religious change. It is just the opposite, he reports, citing data that shows that migrants often attend religious gatherings less often after immigrating to a new country.[11] However, in the case of Guo Kai Li, who had been exposed to the Bible as a child, we can see an example of someone for whom the Bible became very significant almost directly because of her immigrant experience. Guo Kai Li had developed a new identity that merged elements from her preexisting Chinese identity with the new values and critical questions that she began asking as a relatively new immigrant to Canada. While in China, the Bible was insignificant for her. In the diaspora, it became life giving. As identity shifts, meaning and significance with respect to the Bible shift as well.

Yet these shifts betray deep ambiguities. While Christianity invites, it also often sends a message of alienation and denial. The message

---

[10]Phillip Connor, *Immigrant Faith: Patterns of Immigrant Religion in the United States, Canada, and Western Europe* (New York: New York University Press, 2004), 46.

[11]Connor, *Immigrant Faith*, 46-48.

that Canadian Christians had sent her, even if unconsciously, was that Chinese people somehow belong but also are somehow different—are foreign or "pagan." Christianity is never unilingual in its message to immigrants. Nevertheless, Guo Kai Li connected with the stories of the apostle Paul's own hybridity, his multilingualism, and his ambiguity about his Jewish identity vis-à-vis the emerging Jesus groups.[12] Christians who desire to be a part of this dynamic culture will take seriously these ambiguities and work to be agents for hospitality rather than alienation.

My grandmother, Matilda Higuera, was a young girl growing up in Culver City, California in the 1920s. She was a child of an old California family that had kept its Latina/o heritage alive for centuries. She was also a US citizen. During the 1920s and 1930s, she and her family watched helplessly as a growing Anglo-European population swallowed up farm after farm, altering her family's traditional ways of life forever. Her parents had kept alive the memories of California when it was part of Mexico, and they told her stories of Anglo-Europeans seizing family lands by force and state legislation, which had come to be dominated by Anglo-European influences. This legislation failed to protect her family from those seizures.

Because of her experience and the stories that her own grandparents told her, Matilda spent her adult life caring for and looking out for those who crossed the border between the United States and Mexico in search of work. She found new meaning in the language of the Bible that called on God's people to care for the sojourners and the strangers, and she taught her children and grandchildren to treasure those words as well. Her memories of beloved ancestors being victims of hostile Anglo-European border crossings, and of the cataclysm of social change that her family experienced as a result, caused her to understand the sojourner in her world in the same terms as the

---

[12]Tat-Siong Benny Liew, *What Is Asian American Hermeneutics? Reading the New Testament* (Honolulu: University of Hawai'i Press, 2008), 60.

sojourner in the Bible. In this way, she lived in that social space between cultures. Although she lived in the same place as her family had for generations, she found herself living on the borderlands—the cultural borderlands between the California that was emerging and the California of her family's stories around the fireside. Thus, she connected with the new border crossers, whose motives were not to "take" lands from others but to work hard, feed their families, and contribute to their communities. To her, these people were not "wetbacks," as they were commonly called by Anglo-Europeans.[13] They were not "illegal aliens." They were people—people like her—who were suffering discrimination. They were hungry and needed to be fed. They were the biblical sojourners who, like Mary and Joseph in Matthew 2:13-14, like Abraham in Genesis 12 and 26, like the Hebrews in Genesis 47, like Naomi in Ruth 1, and like the prophet Jeremiah, were forced to flee their homelands because of war, destruction, or famine. They were the sojourner on the road who needed a neighbor—a loving Samaritan—to dress their wounds and give them shelter. Because Matilda's own identity was conflicted and hybridized, she and her family always found a way to provide for those sojourners that they encountered. Matilda's Bible read very differently from the Bibles of some Anglo-Europeans, who see migrants and refugees only as a threat and whose social memories have "forgotten" and "erased" the unethical ways that Anglo-Europeans crossed borders and seized lands mere decades before my grandmother was born.

The border wars are very much alive today. For many, the Bible speaks very directly about them. Many of those undocumented who seek to cross the border between Mexico and the United States are descendants of the indigenous local Indians who lived here long before the US Border Patrol or even the Spanish conquest. The lands they cross are traditionally Indian lands—"Cocopah, Papago, Pima,

---

[13]A pejorative term often used to refer to all those who have crossed the border without documents. The term alludes to those who were forced to swim across the Rio Grande and thus arrived in the United States with bodies dripping with water.

Apache, and Yaqui lands."[14] Yet few recognize that those borders were imposed on those indigenous folks in ways that were unjust and that violated accepted human rights norms. Because of this, we can see that the perspective of the one considering border crossings today is crucial in how one interprets those who cross. People of Anglo-European descent might tend to dismiss, justify, ignore, or remain ignorant of this complex history. People of indigenous or Latina/o descent know this history, and, like my Grandma Matilda, it shapes how they respond to border crossings and how they interpret the Bible in light of the stranger, the sojourner, and the pilgrim.

CONCLUDING THOUGHTS

Cultures are not static. They are always in motion. It is because of this that those who reside on the social margins often produce the richest cultural opportunities. Guardians of culture have an interest in the status quo. They do not want to see change because their interests are not served by cultural change. Those on the margins, however, innovate and expand cultural meanings and opportunities as they encounter those changes in their own bodies. Boundaries thus can become both life giving and death dealing. On one hand, cultural boundaries give birth to new musical genres that combine older genres, new literature, new art, new culinary experiments. On the other hand, from the perspective of the powerful, they give birth to fear, xenophobia, alienation, and violence. For this reason, a thoughtful and historically informed notion of hybridity and intersectionality breathes life into hybridized cultures and keeps them—and their people—alive and thriving.

Just as hybridized and diasporic identities keep cultures and people alive, they also keep biblical meaning alive. When the guardians of culture are the only ones who have a voice in interpreting Scripture, then those passages that highlight the plight of the poor and the

---

[14]Luis Alberto Urrea, *The Devil's Highway: A True Story* (New York: Back Bay Books, 2004), 38.

sojourners get overlooked, ignored, suppressed, or viewed as potentially threatening. For the Texas school board members, their own history of state-sponsored terror during slavery and Jim Crow was a threat. For the church fathers, the Jewish people were a threat. For some Anglo-Europeans in the United States today, border crossers are a threat. This is why it is important to bring all voices to the table when interpreting the Bible. Ethnic identities that are hybridized or creolized often open space for recognizing that biblical language itself, when hybridized and creolized, can be life giving. To be blind to these meanings can result in Christians of privilege practicing violence—potentially real as well as social—against their own sisters and brothers in Christ. Hence those who engage in any serious study of the Bible will always consider the identities and social locations of the interpreters, including their own.

It should be central to the academic study of the Bible, then, to consider one's own individual identity as well as the identity of one's group and the ways that those identities shape meaning. But it also needs to be central in home Bible studies, in church Sunday school discussions, and in church leaders' own assessments of how power, identity, culture, and meaning all get constructed within communities of faith.

CONSIDERING THE WHOLE

- Does your family history include a story about migration, exile, or diaspora? How has that story shaped the way you think about your own identity?

- Consider at least one example from your own education in which you realized that your history books shaped the telling of history to reinforce the dominant narrative at the expense of weaker, diasporic groups. How might the weaker group's "restaging" of the history influence cultural meaning?

- What was your understanding of the parable of the loving neighbor (Good Samaritan) before reading this book? Can you make a connection between your own cultural world and how the meaning of the story was conveyed to you?

- Think about two different perspectives you have heard about refugees. Can you identify how different social identities might shape how those different perspectives may have developed?

SUGGESTIONS FOR FURTHER READING

Du Bois, W. E. B. *The Souls of Black Folk*. Rockville, MD: Arc Manor, 2007. First published 1903.

Fredriksen, Paula, and Adele Reinhartz, eds. *Jesus, Judaism, and Christian Anti-Judaism: Reading the New Testament After the Holocaust*. Louisville, KY: Westminster John Knox, 2002.

Matsuda Gruenewald, Mary. *Looking Like the Enemy: My Story of Imprisonment in Japanese American Internment Camps*. Troutdale, OR: NewSage Press, 2005.

Page, Hugh R., Randall C. Bailey, and Valerie Bridgeman et al., eds. *The Africana Bible: Reading Israel's Scriptures from Africa and the African Diaspora*. Minneapolis: Fortress, 2009.

Ruether, Rosemary Radford. *Faith and Fratricide: The Theological Roots of Anti-Semitism*. Eugene, OR: Wipf & Stock, 1995. First published 1974.

Smith, Kay Higuera, Jayachitra Lalitha, and L. Daniel Hawk, eds. *Evangelical Postcolonial Conversations: Global Awakenings in Theology and Praxis*. Downers Grove, IL: IVP Academic, 2014.

Urrea, Luis Alberto. *The Devil's Highway: A True Story*. New York: Back Bay Books, 2004.

Wiesel, Elie. *Night; Dawn; The Accident: A Trilogy*. New York: Hill & Wang, 2004.

7

CONCLUSION

FEDERICO ALFREDO ROTH

IN THEIR 2006 PERSON OF THE YEAR ANNUAL EDITION, the
editors of *Time* magazine broke with years of convention, bestowing
the honor on "You." The cover featured a rectangle in the shape of a
computer monitor fashioned with reflective material and meant to
mirror the image of the beholder. To be sure, *Time* had begun to acknowledge the ways technology had already disrupted traditional
media's structures of power and influence. They recognized how these
forces were fragmenting to form new centers of influence that had
already begun to orbit around the experience of the individual user.
They were right. In the years that have followed that issue, many have
become the creators of their own media content. As a further example
of keen social commentary, the *Time* cover coincides with the decentering of hierarchical ruling bodies in many places and spaces
throughout the world. This book has argued that biblical studies is
one such place. Bible reading has always been a self-reflective enterprise, mirroring the societies and cultures that turn its pages. But only
in recent years have readers grown increasingly aware of this reality.
Our acknowledgment of this fact has been the starting point.

As a reflection of contemporary culture, we have gone beyond simple acknowledgment by working to destabilize the idea that biblical interpretation bears a one-size-fits-all quality. The Bible does not yield its meaning uniformly or singularly. Indeed, the goal of this book has not been to elevate any single strategy for reading above all the rest. One way of reading does not displace, erode, or undermine others. Much to the contrary, the foregoing chapters have shown that no single interpretation should be privileged. Rather, our argument has been that all interpretations, provided they undertake a reasoned engagement with the text, exist to complement one another. Each reading strategy is worthy of consideration, principally because each is poised to see what the others cannot. In so doing, the accumulation of each way of reading offers a fuller, more complete understanding than any one perspective can accomplish on its own.

Moreover, our primary aim has been to celebrate Bible reading as a practice that is thoroughly impacted by those who undertake it. We have learned, then, that biblical studies is not coldly disinterested but *indigenous*, and so shaped by the cultures from which it arises. That is, the study of the Bible will echo the values of a given community and thus reflect that community's unique needs and issues. Knowledge is always conditioned and contextual. The effect of this reality is that readers of the Bible have transitioned from those who receive knowledge to those who construct it. Sweeping designations have given way to concerns that are issue-specific and localized. The Bible has thus emerged as a treasure trove of meaning, able to speak into culture, and through culture, from antiquity to the present day.

WHAT WE'VE LEARNED

The communities represented in the above chapters span the globe. While we have not dared to suggest comprehensive descriptions for ways of reading the Bible, we have taken tentative steps that touch on shared commonalities as we perceive them.

Beginning with Latin America, we first learned that context-based approaches originate from liberation theology. What began as whispers before Vatican II resonated in later ecumenical meetings to move biblical interpretation in an important new direction. Each year since Vatican II proved a decisive step forward for those who sought to interpret the biblical text from the lived experiences of the poor. This angle of inquiry led to the first analysis of the loving neighbor parable. A Latin American reading noticed that the Samaritan migrant brings light and life to a foreign context, breaking cycles of violence and alienation, modeling behaviors that resist injustice, while also demonstrating that insiders and outsiders can, with great courage and kindness, partner to life-saving ends. The reading of Deuteronomy 24:17-22 underscored the multiplicity of vulnerabilities shared among ancient and modern populations and argued favorably for the preservation of dignity among the alien, orphan, and widow, while also serving as a reminder that self-limiting behaviors mimic the kindness of God. The emergence of liberation theology in Latin America, and its attendant ways of reading, would find parallel expressions around the globe. The impact was perhaps most poignantly felt across the Atlantic in Africa.

We learned that African readings will be widely diverse, reflecting the tremendous variance of the continent's many cultural expressions. Notwithstanding this diversity, it is the lived reality of Africa's many people with a commitment to exercising and experiencing liberation, in its many expressions, that forms the bedrock of any Bible reading. So also, it is the shared experience of economic and political exploitation, colonialism (past and present), patriarchy, gender inequalities, class dynamics, and race that together inform any interpretive enterprise. Alice Yafeh's Afro-Cameroonian reading of the loving neighbor parable offers a scriptural model whereby the love of the Samaritan outsider erodes inter/intra-ethnic prejudice, stereotypes, discrimination, and stigma. Tribal relations are thus restructured and reimagined. Here

Jesus teaches that love permeates and transcends rigid social boundaries that would threaten to divide. The analysis of Queens Vashti and
Esther puts in parallel the ways in which interlocking systems of colonial victimization, particularly as related to gender roles and expectations, intersect with the lived experience of Cameroonian women.
Together, Esther and Vashti are elevated as emancipatory resistance
models. African women embroiled in patriarchal structures are re-
sourced with both openly confrontational (Vashti) and secretly subversive (Esther) ways of negotiating their own survival.

Justin Marc Smith moved the conversation to the North Atlantic,
and so to Euro-American approaches. Despite this territory's frac-
tional size, its influence remains vast. These ways of reading Scripture
presuppose that history, and its telling, is an objective reality that can
be discerned through the implementation of prescribed methodological tools. As with other global perspectives, this approach is not
a monolith, splintering into "scientific" and "ambivalent" expressions.
The former embraces the limitations of historical veracity. The latter
argues for scriptural meaning as universal and absolute. As a result, it
enjoys popular support in church communities of this region. When
applied to the loving neighbor parable, a Euro-American reading pro-
duces the general insight that radical love and mercy transcend traditional divisions, be they racial, ethnic, or otherwise. Jesus has enlarged
the meaning of neighbor and neighborliness, but in a way that moves
beyond Samaritan sociocultural identity. Readings of the David and
Bathsheba tale have been less helpful. These have tended to focus on
David as the prime actor, neglecting the character of Bathsheba, her
story of sexual assault, and the added trauma of losing her husband
to satisfy the king's guilt. What is more, she is—with regularity—made
complicit in her own abuse. Euro-American readings have much to
offer those engaged with the Bible on a critical level. However, those
benefits must be counterbalanced with the high cost of its tendency
to depersonalize biblical characters and their stories.

Turning next to Kirsten Sonkyo Oh's discussion, she alerted us to Asia as a geographical space of unparalleled size and scope. The Bible's arrival in Asia, along with its interpretation, was entangled within two complexes. The first set of strictures was imposed by Western missionary ventures, the second by colonial enterprises. By way of example, South Asian readings of the Bible in the colonial era resulted in Orientalist, Anglicist, and Nativist modes of understanding. Among them, the Anglicist model was particularly troubling. In its ardor to discover the Bible's truth as singular, objective, and universal, it left no space for cultural considerations. A pair of recent intellectual shifts have offered more productive possibilities. The first has taken the form of contextual biblical hermeneutics and yielded deeply spiritual readings of biblical texts against the coldly scientific readings of colonizers. The second, postcolonial interpretation, has offered avenues for interrogating Western power and its asymmetrical depictions of East as least while making Asian readers architects of meaning, not simply passive recipients of it. Oh's summary of Asian engagements with the loving neighbor parable has shown that marginal figures are valorized as liberators whose acts of benevolence can transform those who suffer oppression, those who create it as oppressors, and the very systems that would create "Jericho roads" where such distinctions and abuses can occur. Asian readings of Ruth go beyond the issue of gender to identify the multiple and intersecting realities of culture, class, religion, and ethnicity which together ensnare Asian women, but which also provide opportunities for subverting dominant colonial systems.

Kay Higuera Smith's contribution signals a move beyond the geographic categories of previous chapters to highlight how globalization, migration, border crossings and diasporas (both physical and abstract) have served to inform Bible reading and to discern its meaning, often in creative and innovative ways. Smith emphasizes the fluid nature of a reader's multiple and overlapping identities as hybridic, hyphenated, and as a matrix of multiple social and cultural inter-secting points. At times, appreciating one's mosaic of identities in-volves restaging, or resignifying, a particular historical telling from new vantage points that take seriously the stories of marginalized people. Failures to recognize the complexity of human selfhood have led to simplistic readings of the Bible. The parable of the "Good Samaritan," as popularly understood, is an example of this. By "writing out" the subversive and multitextured identity of the Samaritan figure, dominant-culture interpretations make him into a character that is flatly benign, and so unremarkable. We are to focus on his behaviors, not his identity. In such a construal, subversive lessons are forfeited. Lost is the way Jesus is challenging his hearers to confront the status quo, move across predetermined boundaries, and learn from disen-franchised people and their communities. Against this flattening of social and cultural dimensions, Smith has argued that the Bible's meaning can emerge in new and important ways when the reader's experience is not sidelined but invited into the very process of under-standing. For communities of faith that take identity seriously, the Bible can open new life-giving spaces.

Each chapter has modeled novel ways of reading that have invigo-rated our own understanding of what it means to study the Bible. Given the tremendous variety of perspectives active in the world today, the following questions emerge: What will it mean to read the Bible in the days and years to come? What is the profile of the twenty-first century reader? What is the skillset they will need to possess and preserve if they are to continue reading the Bible responsibly, fruitfully, and ethically?

STOP AND THINK

- Consider the summary of reading perspectives in this book. Which one(s) most resonates with your own background and identity? In what ways does it represent your own modes of being and thinking?

- Consider the summary of reading perspectives in this book. Which one is most unlike your own identity? In what ways does it conflict with your own modes of being and thinking?

- Having answered the above prompts, what can each perspective learn from the other? How do they speak to one another? How might they celebrate one another? How might they challenge one another?

- What's missing? What corners of the globe are not covered in the foregoing chapters? What other voices are yet to be heard?

READING THE BIBLE IN THE
TWENTY-FIRST CENTURY

The Bible continues to draw considerable worldwide attention. Its narratives, referents, and themes appear and reappear across a great many cultural landscapes. Reading the Bible has perhaps never been as interesting, producing numerous opportunities for learning. The small sampling of reading approaches presented in this book has given us new optics for seeing and appreciating what biblical interpretation looks like on a global scale. While each perspective stands on its own as a unique expression, they all have contributed to the shape of biblical interpretation as a whole by sharing in at least three important elements. Each perspective models and values (1) self-awareness, (2) Other-awareness, and (3) dialogue. Together they are indispensable features of biblical interpretation that will continue to shape readers and readings for many years to come.

First, contextually sensitive approaches have proven helpful in a variety of important ways. These ways of reading have elevated the important role played by the reader. We have witnessed firsthand the vital function of geographical and social location as energizing forces for determining much of what can be seen (and obscured) in biblical interpretation. It may not be too much to say that the starting point of any theology is the cultural composition of readers themselves. Or, as John J. Vincent has so succinctly put it, "Where you are is who you are."[1] No reading is done in a vacuum, devoid of personal affiliations or commitments. One will read and compute with a set of presuppositions, allegiances, and ideologies that are born from personal and communal histories. The ability to recognize these realities have made self-awareness an indispensable attribute for all readers. We have used geography as the primary organizing element for the foregoing chapters. However, it must be said that land alone is not the only component for constructing the self. Important as it is, the ground beneath one's feet can only be one feature among many for forging understanding. Emerging Bible readers will commit themselves to the practice of ongoing self-assessment and reflection on a multiplicity of fronts.

Additionally, it should be noted that the self-awareness of the reader carries an important protective benefit. We are reminded that a self-reflective posture safeguards biblical interpretation by helping readers to avoid totalizing claims. We have seen much variety in the range of engagements with the parable of the loving neighbor. A simple, linear reading would restrict that story with a fixed and singular, monocultural, meaning for all people in all times. Such a claim would be to erase interpretive diversity, thereby devaluing minority readings, on the one hand, and severely compressing the Bible's message, on the other.

Second, while it is important to cultivate our own innate mode for reading, we must also learn to magnetize ourselves, so to speak— attracting other ways of understanding as well. As such, the above chapters have sought to esteem and encourage an Other-awareness. Here the aim is not to co-opt narratives and histories that are not our own in any disingenuous ways, but to deepen our appreciation of

---

[1] I am indebted to Rev. Dr. John J. Vincent for this insight, delivered in session at the Bible and Justice Conference, Sheffield University, UK, 2008.

them by growing in our sensitivity to them. Readers must undertake such an enterprise owing to the fact that there now exists an expansive spectrum of reading styles, each with its own unique presuppositions, each endowed with its own pitfalls and promises. This now calls for Bible readers to possess an eclectic collection of tools.[2]

Borrowing from Stephanie Mitchem's insightful analogy, the emerging reader of the Bible must venture to resemble the unpredictability and mastery of a jazz musician.[3] Anyone who has ever witnessed a jazz concert knows that at some juncture the musicians will jam. Here the music is intuitive, improvisational, and organic as each member of the band takes a turn at musical expression. Unlike classical music's dependence on sheet music, or better yet, the singular interpretation of the conductor's baton, jazz—particularly when improvised—is a collaborative effort depending on both the *creativity* and *skill* of the individual artist in full partnership with each other. In order to move freely outside the written music, the individual musician must be both supremely skilled with their own instrument and deeply aware of the possibilities and limitations inherent in the instruments of their bandmates.

While a comprehensive understanding of every reading paradigm will be impossible, the goal should be to achieve "informed awareness . . . a working sophistication sufficient enough to follow and interact with a number of particular lines of argumentation, to engage in border crossings so to speak."[4] In short, the aim must be to become conversant with other modes of interpretation. Or, as N. T. Wright has said, "All musicians know, improvisation does not at all

---

[2]Osayande Obery Hendricks describes the volatile nature of his reading style as "guerilla exegesis." "It is transgressive, a transgressive stance, sometimes smooth quick deceptive with pin-point accuracy like Sugar Ray Robinson, sometimes bullish blunt straight-ahead like Joe Frazier. Eclectic. Sometimes float like a butterfly, toe-to-toe in the center of the ring and rope-a-dope-ing all in the same round." See "Guerrilla Exegesis: 'Struggle' as a Scholarly Vocation," in *Semeia*, ed. Janice Anderson Capel and Jeffrey L. Staley, special issue 72 (1995): 79.

[3]Stephanie Y. Mitchem, *Introducing Womanist Theology* (Maryknoll, NY: Orbis, 2002), 78-79.

[4]Mitchem, *Introducing Womanist Theology*, 101.

mean a free-for-all where 'anything goes,' but precisely a disciplined and careful listening to all the other voices around us, and a constant attention to the themes, rhythms and harmonies of the complete performance so far, the performance which we are now called to continue."[5] Bible readers must strive for an intimate awareness of global reading approaches alongside their own.

Third, the emerging trend in the field of biblical studies advances the positive benefits of engagement among the various global perspectives. This is not to suggest that the early years of a new century do not present a great many obstacles to be addressed. For instance, with the increase in specialized reading strategies comes the ever-present fear of isolation and fragmentation among communities who read the Bible for their own purposes. It is conceivable that at some point interaction among approaches will become impossible because the concerns of the various contexts may make such communication a pointless, or needless, exercise. Nevertheless, it is our position that the future of Bible reading will depend on our commitment to fight through the silences inherent in difficult conversation. It will demand that we push for genuine dialogue in order to foster greater appreciation of the Bible's complexities and possibilities. Progress may not be possible without a mutual desire to understand and be understood. The goal of such dialogue will continue to depend on attitudes of openness and mutual humility. Those residing in places and spaces of privilege will have to travel to the margins just as those on the margins will have to take tentative steps toward the center. These conversations will need to take place at tables with rounded corners, where all engage in active listening and all voices speak with shared authority, agency, and dignity.

The profile of the emerging Bible reader not only appreciates dialogue for its own sake, but actively works to facilitate it among others.

---

[5]N. T. Wright, *The Last Word: Scripture and the Authority of God—Getting Beyond the Bible Wars* (New York: HarperCollins, 2005), 93.

They are in a constant search to build networks and bridges between would-be dialogue partners. This is a cultivated ability to speak one's own language as it is the ability to speak in many tongues, at times undertaking considerable risk. These will function like translators of sorts, creating space for the exchange of ideas from person to person and community to community.

STOP AND THINK

- Consider the qualities detailed above. Which of the three presents the biggest blind spot for you? Why do you suppose that is?

- In what ways do you believe you have grown in your self-awareness as a Bible reader? What presuppositions and commitments have you discovered in your own thinking?

- In what ways have you grown as an "Other-aware" reader of the Bible? How have you learned to see the world through another's eyes?

- In what ways do you, or have you, fostered dialogue among different ways of reading the Bible?

CONCLUDING THOUGHTS

The written work of political activist and theorist Antonio Gramsci stands among the most significant of the twentieth century. Imprisoned under Italy's Fascist regime from 1929 to 1935, Gramsci's now-famous *Prison Notebooks* feature a collection of essays on a wide array of social topics. In one instance, Gramsci muses on the nature of human selfhood, concluding that history marks the individual with an "infinity of traces" for which no orderly inventory exists. Gramsci suggests that the human task is, therefore, to organize this inventory of identity not by looking within to one's inner self, but by turning outward. According to Gramsci, to know oneself one must strive to know one's other. It is only by imagining ourselves *as* others—and in a sense becoming someone we are not—that we may arrive at self-knowledge.[6] Life is paradoxical insofar as we understand ourselves by understanding those around us. As Edward Said, the noted cultural critic, has similarly commented, "No identity is pure, everyone counter, original, spare, strange. . . . We are all Others in the final analysis."[7] These insights on the nature of selfhood correspond with changes already well underway in biblical studies.

Global perspectives represent an inversion of business-as-usual norms in biblical scholarship. For too many years, the Euro-American mode for reading called for a disconnected and disinterested interpreter, immune from personal histories, whether those of others or of themselves. The ideal reader was a technician, equipped to follow procedures and adept at excising meaning *from* the Bible. Theology was, therefore, largely untethered from human experience and little more than a cognitive undertaking done *by* specialists *for* specialists. To think theologically was, by definition, to be numbered among the elites. Well-intentioned as it was, such study was the preserve of experts whose focus was typically to determine a singular meaning. By reducing possibilities for understanding, it impoverished the inherent value of the biblical text, circumscribing it in restrictive ways.

The global perspectives represented in this book have offered a different roadmap forward. These new ways of understanding function as an invitation for Bible readers—particularly those at home in places of power and privilege—to engage in a kind of "theological tourism," as it were.[8] Bible readers in the twenty-first century would do well to

---

[6]Antonio Gramsci, *Prison Notebooks*, ed. J. A. Buttigieg, 3 vols. (New York: Columbia University Press, 2011). See especially vol. 2.

[7]Speech given at Mount Hermon school, quoted in William V. Spanos, *The Legacy of Edward W. Said* (Urbana: University of Illinois Press, 2009), 231.

[8]Mary Ann Tolbert uses this term to describe the process by which First World readers experience the vitality of Christian experience as communicated by those of the Two-Thirds World. See "Afterwords: Christianity, Imperialism, and the Decentering of Privilege," in *Reading from This Place*, vol. 2, *Social Location and Biblical Interpretation in Global Perspective*, ed. Fernando F. Segovia and Mary Ann Tolbert (Minneapolis: Fortress, 1995), 354.

traverse the biblical canon in such a way that will cultivate open-handed curiosity and a certain appreciation of eclecticism, not expertise. They would do well to strain for appreciation, not possession. Perhaps what is now needed are not more experts, but rather "amateurs," in the etymological sense of the word. That is, those who authentically and enthusiastically exhibit a "love of" knowledge, especially if that knowledge comes through the eyes of others.

CONSIDERING THE WHOLE

- Which of the global perspectives represented in the book's chapters most resonate with your own reading of the Bible? Why do you think that's so?

- Which of the global perspectives represented in the book's chapters present challenges for you? What are they?

- What do you anticipate are places for further study and discovery? What still puzzles you?

- Can you detect any additional benefits to global approaches? If so, what are they?

SCRIPTURE INDEX

Finding the Textbook You Need

The IVP Academic Textbook Selector
is an online tool for instantly finding the IVP books
suitable for over 250 courses across 24 disciplines.

---

ivpacademic.com